MW01591016

공 정식 목사님께

The Pilgrimage to Heaven

How to Have Eternal Life and Enter Heaven

김정태

John C. T. Kim

iUniverse, Inc.
Bloomington

The Pilgrimage to Heaven
How to Have Eternal Life and Enter Heaven

Bible quotations are taken from the HOLY BIBLE, NEW INTERNATIONAL VERSION®. Copyright © 1973, 1978, 1984 by International Bible Society. Used by permission of Zondervan Publishing House. All rights reserved.

iUniverse books may be ordered through booksellers or by contacting:

iUniverse
1663 Liberty Drive
Bloomington, IN 47403
www.iuniverse.com
1-800-Authors (1-800-288-4677)

Because of the dynamic nature of the Internet, any web addresses or links contained in this book may have changed since publication and may no longer be valid. The views expressed in this work are solely those of the author and do not necessarily reflect the views of the publisher, and the publisher hereby disclaims any responsibility for them.

Any people depicted in stock imagery provided by Thinkstock are models, and such images are being used for illustrative purposes only.

Certain stock imagery © Thinkstock.

ISBN: 978-1-4759-6521-6 (sc)
ISBN: 978-1-4759-6523-0 (hc)
ISBN: 978-1-4759-6522-3 (e)

Library of Congress Control Number: 2012922741

Printed in the United States of America

iUniverse rev. date: 12/27/2012

Dedicated to
the seekers of God, eternal life, and heaven

Contents

Preface

We all love eternal life, desire it, and pursue it. When we obtain it, we have life and enter heaven. We are in bliss. But when we forfeit it, we die and perish in hell. We are in distress.

This book compiles an account of my pilgrimage to heaven. After seventy years of my journey to heaven through the world, I look back the ways I have walked and the lives I have entered. Once I descended into the abyss of death and hell. Now I am walking on the path of life and heaven.

The things written in this book are not a philosophical essay about the secret of life or a theological treatise on the mystery of God. I am neither a philosopher nor a theologian. The understanding of God and life has come to me by the revelations of Jesus Christ. Through many revelations and visions, I have seen both the way of man and the way of God and their life conditions. Having experienced hell and heaven on my pilgrimage, I am eager to tell you my testimonies to God and life. I bear witness to the things that I have heard, seen, and experienced so that you also may have life and enter heaven.

This book is intended primarily for the souls that are seeking God, eternal life, and heaven. Men and women in a wretched, miserable, sinful state are searching for God in their trouble. The lost are yearning to be found by God. The dead are longing for life. The perishing are desperately crying out for help, for there is none to help them in the world. They ask in their distress, "What shall I do to have eternal life?" The book shows how I found God and eternal life out of my distress of perishing in hell. In addition, those who have heard of God and wish to experience Him and His life will benefit from the book.

As disclaimers, the author and publisher offer the following warnings: First, this book is written for the poor in spirit. The rich in this world may be disturbed by what the book has to say. Where do you turn for help when your life is in trouble? Human wisdom (e.g., theology, philosophy, psychology, medical science) will not help; the problems of sin and death are too difficult for man to solve. You need a miracle—the miracle of God. For the help of God, you must turn to Jesus Christ. The way of God is different from yours. Second, the book deals with the truth of God. Those who oppose the truth can be offended by it. Having the truth in my heart, I proclaim Him boldly. I was not taught the truth by human wisdom but received the gift of God through Jesus Christ. And I am human like you. Consequently, I feel far from any sense of superiority. I am under obligation to you and declare the truth with humility and in weakness. The information in the book is written for your good. Blessed is the one who keeps from stumbling over the truth. The author and publisher hereby disclaim all liability for any loss or damage related to the book.

The author gratefully acknowledges the help of kind persons. My daughter Naomi reviewed the draft of this book and made suggestions for writing good English. Mitch Fairrais, my friend and president of On the Mark, read the manuscript with cheerfulness and provided valuable insight. My wife, God-given helper, enabled me to make time to write the book.

Toronto, Canada
Autumn 2012

Introduction

God promised the life in Jesus Christ to mankind. According to the promise of God, we hope for eternal life. Our vision is the true, heavenly life placed by God before us. We look forward to entering heaven and possessing the good life of God.

Our lives in this world are pilgrimages to the promised life of God in heaven. Heaven is the destination of the journey of human life. (The destiny of human life is not death. Nor is the grave the terminus of our journeys in the world. No one lives to go to hell.) We are on the journey to heaven, the country of God, where all is peace, love, joy, and glory. In fact, all of us already set out on the pilgrimage to heaven.

One important question that we face in undertaking the journey of life to heaven, as in any journey, is this: How shall we reach our destination? In the pilgrimage to heaven, we go through the wilderness of the world where there are no paths to eternal life and heaven. And none of us had ever passed through the world before. Knowing the right way will help us enter heaven successfully and ensure us enjoy our pilgrimages along the way.

God's promise in Jesus Christ presents two ways before us. One is the way of unbelief. At the times of ignorance, we are unwilling to believe in Jesus Christ. (If we knew Jesus Christ and the gift of God, we would have come to Him for eternal life and heaven.) We turn away from Jesus Christ and set out for the world by our own ways. We pursue eternal life and heaven as if they were attained by our own works in the world. Most people attempt the pilgrimage to heaven along the way of man in the world. I also once was one of them.

The other way is the way of belief. Those who believe in Jesus Christ seek eternal life and heaven by the faith and hope in Him. The believers follow Jesus Christ, who descended from heaven to the world and then ascended into heaven through death and resurrection. Only a minority finds the way of God in Jesus Christ.

The four parts of this book compare and contrast the two ways and their respective lives and final destinations.

Part One: The Way of Man

1. Man's Thoughts in Unbelief

The Unbelieving
> The Revelations of God to Man
> The Unbelieving
> The Symptoms of Unbelief

The Nearsighted and Blind

The Ignorant and Speculating
> The Wise of the World
> No Knowledge of the Lord God
> No Knowledge of the World
> No Self-knowledge
> No Knowledge of Life
> Speculating in the Darkened Heart

The Misguided and Separated
> The Misguided by the World
> The Deceived by Sin
> The Separated from God
> The Exiled from the Life of God

This chapter examines man's unbelieving heart and considers the unbeliever's thoughts on God, the world, man, and life.

The Unbelieving

The Revelations of God to Man

Since the beginning of the world, the God of heaven has performed His signs and manifested His glory before all men and women. Opening the Bible, we hear an amazing thing about God: "In the beginning God created the heavens and the earth." The Bible declares that God made the world.

The world clearly reveals the divine nature of the Creator God. Look at the world of God's creation and see His signs as the Lord

God. The natural world displays the eternal wisdom and power of God. When the majestic mountains and grand valleys of the Canadian Rockies call us to honor and worship the God of creation, we stand in awe of the Creator. We see the wonders of God in nature and say with the sense of mystery, "Wonderful!"

Indeed, God made us wonderfully. Ask a medical doctor about how human body is made in the forms and functions of its many parts, an ophthalmologist about human eyes, and a dentist about human teeth. They will bear witnesses of the greatness of God's wisdom and power. And you will marvel at the wonders of God.

God has revealed His glory in the creation of the world, so that we might seek Him, find the Lord (the sovereign Master as the Maker of the world) of creation, and know that the Lord is our God.

In addition to His revelations in the natural world, the God of heaven has shown His righteousness and justice in His judgments against man's sinfulness. When Adam and Eve disobeyed the word of God, they were exiled from the Garden of Eden and suffered death. At the time of Noah, God judged the ancient world of the ungodly with a great flood. He destroyed the cities of Sodom and Gomorrah to ashes when the citizens sinned. He punished the sinful people of Israel at the times of the Old Testament of the Bible with foreign occupations and exiles.

When Jonah, a prophet of Israel, fled from the presence of God on a ship, the Lord of the world raised up a great storm on the sea. He and the sailors became extremely frightened and perceived the presence of God in the calamity. When we see such a storm as we have never seen before, that our souls melt away in our peril, we fear the wrath of God on our sins. The storm of an unusual magnitude brings our sinfulness to remembrance. We come to know that sinners will not escape the righteous judgment of God.

The judgments of God abide on not only murderers and adulterers but also the scoffers and mockers saying, "Where is the judgment of God?" There are pain and distress for all evildoers. All over on the earth, we see sufferings and death and hear mourning and crying.

In His judgments for our sins, God remembers His promise of life in Jesus Christ. He has revealed His grace for sinners through Jesus

Christ. Our hope for eternal life has been revealed by the appearing of our Savior Jesus. He performed many miracles and manifested the glory of God for us to know the Lord and Savior and believe in Him for the salvation of God.

This is the word of God we hear. We respond to it with either belief or unbelief. The believers rejoice in the God of salvation because their sins are forgiven and they have eternal life. In contrast, the unbelievers suppress the word of God and reject the gift of eternal life and heaven in Jesus Christ.

The Unbelieving

Despite all the miraculous signs that God has performed before our eyes, we would not believe in the Lord our God. We saw the glory of God in the natural world and the judgments of God on the earth and heard the word of God's salvation. But we refused to repent and turn to our God for the forgiveness of sin and eternal life. We made our hearts harder than stone and disbelieved Jesus Christ. And we despised the precious word of God without knowledge.

God has made Himself known in His works, so that we might honor, worship, and serve the Lord our God for His blessed life. Nevertheless, we worship and serve other gods in our own ways. The nations of the world make their own gods and serve them according to their cultures and traditions. Generally, Westerners serve the Judeo-Christian God; the Arabs, Allah; and Asians, Buddha or Brahman.

I was born in Busan, Korea, in November 1941. My father seemed to me to have need of nothing from God for his life. My mother was a cultural Buddhist and visited the temples in the mountains twice a year. It was impressive for me to watch from a distance her washing herself in the stream in the mountains to appear before Buddha. Early in the mornings, she used to go to the altar prepared in the back garden of our house with a bowl of clean water. Looking up to the heaven, she offered prayers to her god for me to have success in the world.

My parents taught me nothing about the God of heaven. Instead, they brought me up in the discipline and instruction of manliness. They used to teach me by saying, "Man shall be like man and live unlike animals." My father loved me so much that he did not spare me from the rod of discipline when I went my ways of curiosity and carelessness. It was a humbling experience to prepare my own rods from the branches of poplars near our house. My mother diligently trained me to discern personal characters from the styles of walking. I have two sisters and one brother. We have never had any conflictive experiences with our parents or one another.

My grandmother served the god of the mountain. She loved to take me to her place of worship in the deep mountains. An altar was built in front of two large boulders standing tall and leaning against each other. She declared that the mighty spirit of her god dwells in the tiger living in the cave of the boulders. While she prepared her sacrifices of food on the altar and worshiped her god, I, a small boy, trembled with extreme vigilance in the fear of a tiger.

The people of the community called my grandmother "tiger grandma." The nickname was given partly because she worshiped the tiger in her holy mountain and partly because she was a tiger-eyed disciplinarian in the community. She was stern and fearsome in disciplining the community people and her grandson. By her example and instructions, she taught me about fearing her god and about human behaviors from good table manners to uprightness in both body and mind.

While I was still a boy, I used to hear the church bells ringing from some distance. But they were no more than a reminder that it was Sunday. When I heard the word of Jesus saying, "If someone strikes you on the right cheek, turn to him the other also," I could not understand His strange teaching. It was quite contrary to my nature. I did not believe the word of Jesus; it was foolishness to me.

The Symptoms of Unbelief

Now, what happens to us when we do not believe in Jesus Christ, the word of God? We are condemned to death. We die spiritually and later physically. Our dead hearts are hard and senseless like calluses.

The unbelieving heart is hearing-impaired. The ears of the heart are stopped with the plug of unbelief, which disables them from hearing the word of God. We are deaf spiritually. We keep on hearing the word of God with our ears, but it cannot enter our stopped hearts. And we do not understand the word of God with our hearts.

The hardened heart is also dull of spiritual perception. It is covered with the veil of unbelief. The light of God's glory cannot enter our hearts; there is deep darkness in our hearts. The eyes of our hearts abide in the blinding darkness of death. Although we have eyes, we cannot see the revelations of God. We are unable to see the wonderful things of God. We keep on looking at the signs of God but cannot see the glory of God with our hearts. While seeing the miracles of God, we do not perceive His signs. We are visually impaired. We are on the journey to life and heaven but do not know where we are going.

Furthermore, our senseless hearts are obstinate. The doors of our hearts are tightly shut by the disobedience of unbelief. With the stronghold of unbelief, we stubbornly refuse to listen to the word of God. We are determined not to acknowledge God. In fact, we are hostile toward God.

For this reason, we could not believe.

The Nearsighted and Blind

The unbelievers, having the darkened heart, are nearsighted and blind. They can see as far as their physical eyes see—that is, the nearsighted see only the visible side of the world. The invisible side of the world is beyond the range of their eyesight. The nearsighted can see the natural things of the world, but the blind cannot see the spiritual things of God; earthly things, but not heavenly things; and the appearance of the world, but not the reality of God. They are unable to perceive the things the eyes of the heart see, for example, the way, the truth, and the life of God. They are blind spiritually. The nearsighted see in part and know in part.

In my boyhood, I enjoyed observing the sky, the mountains, and the ocean in my beautiful hometown, Busan. I heard of other cities behind the mountains, foreign countries over the ocean, and heaven beyond the sky, but I could not see them. My eyesight ended where the mountains met the sky and ships vanished beneath the far horizon. My heart longed to see the unseen world yonder, and the only thing I could do was to dream about the world beyond the limit of my vision.

The world I knew was what I could see with my eyes. The bounds of my view of the world were the end of my comprehension. Like a frog in a deep well, I was closed up to my small world. I could not see the wide world outside of my vision. The world beyond my sight was an enigma.

I perceived things as they appeared. I viewed the world as a small boy and thought childish things. I believed the earth is flat like a playground; that was the way the earth appeared to me on the horizon. The concept that the earth is round like a ball was a puzzle for me. I was not yet able to see the globe as astronauts see it. My small mind was baffled with the notion that the enormous globe, with all things on it, floats in space and revolves around the sun while rotating by itself. My mind inquired in amazement and perplexity, "How is it possible for the rotating earth to contain the ocean water? With the earth upside-down, how can I still stand on the top of the earth?" The earth was beyond my comprehension and imagination. Great was the mystery of the world.

Time is a straight line having a beginning and an end. Time runs its course towards its end. Therefore, all things of the world are temporal and perishable. A person's life on the earth ends. The time line has the past, the present, and the future. A particular period of time (e.g., a day, a year, a century) is a point on the time line. The repeating rounds of days and years are the points in the linear course of time. The connected points make a line of time.

Nevertheless, I, a nearsighted boy, watched the repeating rounds of days, seasons, and years, and thought the world as an endless cycle to be everlasting. I had no prospect of the day of my death and the end of the world and thought that I will live on for a long, long time, perhaps five hundred years.

Observing that the people around me loved me, I, a naïve boy, assumed that the world is all about me. I thought that I was the center of the world, and that people should pay attention to me only. I, a spoiled boy, expected that people should serve me, and looked out for my own interests only. I, a nearsighted and blind boy, could see no one beyond myself. I was self-centered and selfish.

The nearsighted by unbelief have their views about almost everything. They believe they have insight and understanding, but they do not know that they are nearsighted and blind. While seeing the things perceptible to their physical senses, they cannot see the truth and life of God.

Unbelieving scientists think that the truth will be found in nature, as they see further and deeper into nature than common people do. They have insight into their fields, but their insight has the limit of nearsightedness. They look at things as they appear, and they cannot see the true reality beyond scientific facts observable by their physical senses. Since scientific discoveries are gained through natural, empirical observations, scientists have nearsighted knowledge of the truth. Scientific researchers suggest theories, not the truth, to explain natural phenomena. They deny the truth of God, which is beyond their sights and scientific evidences. They would not accept the things of God, which are beyond their understanding. The scientists without the knowledge of the truth grope in darkness with the dim lamp of their theses and hypotheses.

Nearsighted scientists keep on observing nature, but they cannot perceive the supernatural things such as the Lord God and creation. They look into the earth, the sky, the ocean, plants, animals, and humans, but do not see the Lord of all these things. They explore the creation of God but cannot catch a glimpse of the God of creation. Nature points to the One who created it, but the blind scientists cannot see the Creator God beyond the nature. Some scientists believe the existence of God but are troubled with His creation. Anything beyond the apparent evidences established by scientific methods is a mystery to them.

Nature appears evolution by sight, but it is creation in truth. Nearsighted biologists observe evolution but do not perceive creation.

Scientific perception is not capable of observing the whole of things. The creation of God is beyond their sight and is a mystery to them.

Creation and evolution are simply two ways of looking at the same object of the nature. One way is by spiritual eyes through faith; the other, by natural eyes through scientific methods. While scientists look at the phenomena of evolution in nature, the eyes of the believers see the reality of God the Creator beyond the nature. The different perspectives are considered mutually exclusive and have caused worthless antagonism between creationists and evolutionists. Both sides should realize that evolution is a scientific fact and creation is a transcendent truth. Science tells us about the outward appearance of things, whereas the truth shows us the ultimate nature of things. Therefore, there is no need for controversies and arguments to prove their one-sided views. And Christian faith should not be shaken by scientific discoveries, nor should scientists be skeptical about the truth of God.

Biochemists experiment with living things but do not discover eternal life in them. Physicists can split an atom to see mighty energy but cannot make the power of God for godliness and life. Astronomers observe the sky but cannot see heaven through their scientific methods.

I myself was a student of science. Trees were the objects of my observation. I beheld many wonderful things about trees: the new life from seeding, cutting, and grafting; the beauty of a tree and the forest in changing seasons; the perfect arrangement of branches, leaves, and flowers; and deciduous trees losing their colorful leaves before winter and coniferous leaves surviving the frigid winter. In my many years of researching trees and wood, I observed the intricacies of how all things work in the life of a tree and the complexities of how wood was physically and chemically linked. The physical structure and chemical distribution giving a tree enough strength to stand under gravity and the wind kept me marveling. I was amazed by the wonders of trees and wood, and used to exclaim in awe, "Marvelous!"

Despite all the evidences of God's creation, I could not see the God of the wonders. I kept observing the creatures of God but could not perceive the Creator who is behind nature. Nature displayed the almighty works of God before my eyes, but I, being blinded by unbelief, could not see God.

The desire of my heart throughout my scientific researches was to find something nobody else had discovered before. But that was hard for me, a blind man. I researched nature to find the truth along my theses, feeling about aimlessly for my way in darkness. Struggling with the truth and nature of wood, I was lost in the unapproachable wisdom and power of God.

While watching seasons come and go and trees grow taller, I could not see my personal growth. I thought I had a vision of life, but in reality I was nearsighted and blind. Without insight into the mystery of life, I looked for the way to life in the wrong place—in nature. I walked in the dark and had no idea where I was going. I groped in deep darkness to feel my way to life.

Philosophers search for the truth about man and the wisdom of life. Through philosophy, they try to answer the questions: "What is man? What is life? What is the meaning of life?" (The Greek word *philosophia,* from which the English word "philosophy" derives, denotes the love of wisdom.) Wisdom lovers pursue the truth and nature of life with their intelligences. They look into their own minds to obtain a deeper insight into life. But they are not able to find the wisdom for eternal life in their darkened hearts. The wisdom of God for life is veiled to the wise of the world.

The religious people without the Spirit of truth have heard of God with their ears, but the eyes of their darkened hearts have never seen Him. Since all sinners are in the darkness of death, they cannot see God. They seek the God of heaven but cannot find Him through their religions, creeds, or traditions. The people of worldly religions cannot see God or understand His works. For instance, when Jesus said to Nicodemus, a teacher of Jews in the Bible, "No one can enter the kingdom of God unless he is born of water and the Spirit," he marveled. He could not see how the born of man can be reborn of God. Spiritual birth after natural birth was beyond his sight and understanding. The Samaritan woman at Jacob's well in the Bible also could not understand when Jesus taught about the living water out of heaven springing up to eternal life. All she could see was the natural water drawn from the well. When Jesus opened the eyes of a blind man from birth in the Bible, the Jews could not see how the blind man received sight. The onlookers saw the miracle but could not see the sign of Jesus as the Savior of the world. The Pharisees (a Jewish party observing the Law zealously and literally) looked at the law of God on the Sabbath, but they could not recognize their Messiah Jesus giving sight to the blind.

Some religious people today see the letter of Moses' law on the Sabbath, but they cannot see the Lord of the Sabbath who fulfilled the law for us. They know the law on food in the Old Testament of the Bible but do not know the grace of God in Jesus Christ who declared that all foods are clean. They do not understand that the kingdom of God is not eating but the righteousness in the Holy Spirit.

Nearsighted and blind theologians search the Bible systematically but do not find the God of the Bible, just as biologists dissect a frog for their researches and no longer see the frog. By feeling different parts of God or focusing on various verses of the Scriptures, they emphasize strange doctrines and practices for Christianity. For example, Calvinists see the absolute sovereignty of God and the total depravity of man, but they do not see the grace of God in Jesus Christ for all sinners to behold the Son of God and believe in Him. In contrast, Arminians see the grace of God and the free will of man and become blind. They cannot see the things Calvinists see. Can a sinner repent and believe at the sinner's own free will? The sinner with a depraved heart can do nothing apart from the Helper, the Holy Spirit. Conversely, can a person freely refuse to believe in Jesus Christ when the Holy Spirit works in the person with the power and glory of God? No, the person in the presence of God does nothing but respond to Him with belief. Believing in Jesus Christ is not the work of man done by a free will choice but a human response to the works of the Holy Spirit. Many Charismatics stress the Pentecostal experiences of the filling with the Holy Spirit and speaking in different tongues (other languages) in the Bible, Acts 2:4, but they do not see other passages in the Bible on the phenomena of the Holy Spirit.

We see that people are born, grow old, and die, and that most of them do not know where they are going in life or in death. The darkness of unbelief has blinded their eyes; they cannot see the way to heaven. How can they find the way to eternal life when they are blind and ignorant?

The Ignorant and Speculating

The Wise of the World

We all have knowledge, but not all have the knowledge of the truth. (The goal of knowledge is to know the truth, Jesus Christ.) The truth according to Jesus Christ is known by faith, not by human wisdom. For this reason, the unbelievers are ignorant of the truth, however knowledgeable they are.

During my tender teen years, I was fascinated with life in my body. The body has many parts and each part has its own form and function. Looking at my body disconnected from the world but still alive as an individual, I wondered about the source of life, "What animates my body? Where does the life-giving power come from?"

To find the power of life, I looked at my body and examined breath and the respiratory system. I knew the body needs to breathe for life, but life dies by severe bleeding. So I turned to blood in the body. A person with blood can still die with circulation problems. Then I inquired about what powers for circulation. Coming to the heart and searching for the force for pumping blood in the heart, I realized I could not find the source of blood pressure in the body. My search was at an impasse when I reached the realm of the unseen things.

Soon after the search, I got the idea that a person of knowledge has the wisdom and power for life. And I set my heart to increase knowledge and started to read books on human life and ethics. Some words drew my attention, and I meditated on them to gain the wisdom of life.

In my quest for understanding and wisdom during my adolescence, I gathered knowledge from classical literature, natural science, and oriental and occidental philosophy by reading many books and much studying.

My zeal for knowledge brought tearfulness to my mother. She loved having me near her and wished me to go to a university in my hometown. When I left her to study at a reputable university far away from home, she went out to the fields to weep away every day, looking up at the northern sky above where I was. Her tears finally dried up after five months.

While majoring forestry at Seoul National University in Korea, I was intensely interested in various schools of philosophy and thoughts. Great thinkers of human history were in my mind and their thoughts were my meditations. At the weekly Wednesday meetings held at his house, Professor Yu Dal-young taught us about Christian (non-church) thought and Confucianism. To explore more about Christianity, I attended a Roman Catholic church near the university for a few Sundays.

When it was time to enter the world after university graduation, I tried to put all my knowledge together and speculated a way by which I should walk to have a good life in the world.

None of my knowledge, however, taught my heart to know the wisdom and power of God for eternal life. Instead, my much knowledge puffed me up to believe that I know all things and can do all things. The haughtiness of my pride lifted me up to believe in myself. Being self-sufficient, I felt no personal need of God and did not seek Him. God and spiritual things lay outside my view and interest. My arrogance assumed that God and religions are for the weak and the foolish.

Whenever, though occasionally, I heard about Jesus Christ, I did not even attempt to inquire about Him but rejected Him in hostility. Without knowing the precious value of Jesus Christ, I spurned the power and wisdom of God for godliness and life. He was beyond my knowledge and understanding. I suppressed the truth in unbelief and refused to have God in my knowledge. Even though I loved knowledge and pursued the truth, I hated God. The result was that I was always learning but did not come to the knowledge of the truth. My darkened heart was unable to distinguish true from false, right from wrong, or good from evil. I was ignorant about the higher things of God and the deeper things of my soul.

The unbelieving heart has no knowledge of the truth about God, the world, man, and life.

No Knowledge of the Lord God

The ignorant of God say, "Where is God?" They dare to declare, "There is no God." They revile the majestic things of God about which they have no knowledge. God is holy and is hidden in a mystery. The unbelieving and sinful people cannot see or know Him. They have no reverential fear of God before their eyes and blaspheme the holy name of God. God is spirit and invisible. And they believe God, who is not seen, does not exist.

Truly, there is God. Although there are many so-called gods in the world, there is only one God. The Lord of heaven and earth is our God, and there is no other. The unbelievers do not have this knowledge. They know neither who the true Lord is nor who the true God is.

People of worldly religions somehow believe the existence of God and search after Him to find Him. But they have not yet known the Lord God, as they ought to know. They worship a strange God and serve Him in ignorance.

Theology, human science or knowledge of God, cannot reach heaven or know God in a mystery. Who among us can ascend into heaven by theology and find God? God is in heaven; we are on the earth. We are finite; God is infinite. No matter how high we build our own towers with theological knowledge, we cannot reach heaven or come to know God by the human wisdom. God is holy and transcendent. Only through the revelation of Jesus Christ and by faith, we can see the glory of God and come to understand the Lord our God. The knowledge of God is hidden from the unbelievers.

Three significant events in my youth occurred during my graduate student years at the University of British Columbia, Vancouver, Canada. First, I learned through my scientific researches into nature that there is a supernatural Being, an invisible and almighty power, beyond the nature. In one way or another I sensed that the spirit of the Supreme Being in a mystery was filling the universe. Second, I met two Christians, David and Ruby Hayward, who deeply impressed me by their manners of life. They gave me my first Bible and took me to Trinity Baptist Church in Vancouver on several Sundays. At the church I heard the word of God but could not comprehend it at all. Third, I married a Christian. My wife, Grace, kept telling me that the supernatural Being is the Lord God. But I vehemently disputed with her by saying, "Your God is not my Supreme Being."

No Knowledge of the World

We must know the Lord God to know the world in truth. The nearsighted knowledge of the world is partial. The world is not all that it appears: it is much more than what the unbelievers know. Beyond the natural, visible world, there is the spiritual, invisible world. The unbelievers do not know about the eternal world after the temporal world; it is hidden from them. The true, heavenly country of God is beyond their comprehension.

At the times of ignorance, we believe the world is for us—to grab it as ours. We strive to gain it for our own kingdom and life because we do not know that the world was created by the Lord our God and for Him. Nor do we understand that we live through Him and for Him.

My ignorance was obvious in my error of loving and serving the world rather than the Lord God of the world. I knew nothing about the world in true judgment. As though the world belonged to me, I sought wealth, position, and pleasures in the world for my life and glory. I had grab-everything approaches to the world. Sitting on the throne of my heart was not the Lord my God but I. I was the king of my life and the judge of the world and sought my own kingdom and justice. I followed what was right in my own eyes. But I, an ignorant king, did not know why I am in the world, what I should do for life and glory, where I am going, or how I should walk in the world to enter heaven.

Also, I was not sure of my identity as a citizen in the world. Becoming a Canadian citizen, I was confused about my country. The documents issued by the Canadian government say that I am a Canadian. But the people of Canada look at my physical appearance and say that I am a Korean. Meanwhile, whenever I visit Korea, I feel like a foreigner in my homeland. Since I emigrated from Korea in 1970, the country, the land, the people, and the culture—all have changed so much that I have become a stranger in my old country. I have changed too. I feel I do not belong to any country in the world. If I do not have my citizenship in the country of heaven, what a personal identity crisis I would have to go through! Truly, I am a pilgrim in the world. My—and your—true homeland is heaven.

Moreover, the unbelievers have no knowledge of the spiritual, invisible forces of evil in the world. They are unaware of the existence of Satan, the Devil. The world is under the dominion of Satan, the god of this world. Satan tempts man to sin against God; the man of the world has enmity against God. There are demons, the servants of Satan, in the air. The activities of Satan and demons work for the destruction of man. Hence, there are spiritual conflicts in the world. We must understand what the deceitful schemes of Satan are, and resist the spiritual forces of evil in the world. If we do not keep watching and praying, Satan will devour us to destruction and ruins.

No Self-knowledge

An ancient philosopher counseled, "Know thyself." But we still query, "Who am I? What am I?" We inquire, "Where did man come from?"

In the years of my ignorance, I did not know my origin. When I came to Canada as an immigrant, people asked me, "Where did you come from?" Thinking of that country from which I came, I answered, "I came from Korea." When I was asked about my origin beyond my people, I was lost in darkness. A Korean myth told us that Koreans came from a bear. Now I know for sure that I did not come from the animal. All of us, Jews and Gentiles, originally came from God.

Nonetheless, the wise of the world link humans with animals and have pride as highly developed or evolved animals. They should know that we are humans, not animals. The right answers to our questions about man come not from human wisdom but from the word of God, our Maker.

In the beginning God made a man and a woman. We were born to be the sons and daughters of God. Although we do not appear as what we are in truth, we are the children of God. The children of men and women know their parents. Dogs recognize their masters. But the unbelieving children of God do not know their Father in heaven.

The ignorant children of God live like orphans, all alone in the universe. The heirs of the Lord God of heaven and earth worry about what to eat, what to wear, and where to dwell for life. Though they are dying with hunger and thirst in the world far from their Father, the ignorant children have no place to go. When they are in distress, they do not know where to turn to for help.

What is man like? The ignorant wish to be like rich and famous men and women. Women with yellow skin and black hair desire to be like Caucasians with white skin and blonde hair. On the other hand, Caucasians like to have tanned and brown skin.

Now, let us turn to our Maker and see what man is truly like. Our Maker God has bestowed His image and likeness on us, so that we should become partakers of His nature. Humanity is the representation of God's nature, that is, we have filial resemblance to God the Father. We are the likeness of God according to His image: we are the image and glory of God. The potential of man is to be like God. Our Father in heaven calls us to be like Him. We are to be perfect, as our heavenly Father is perfect. To be man is to be like God, the holy One. To be human is to be godly. A person conformed to the image and glory of God is a perfect person.

The question what kind of person I am can be answered by the definition of man described above. A person has infinite value as the image of God, over the person's achievements, possessions, and fame in the world. If I am somebody of the boastful pride with the glory of the world but do not bear the likeness after the image of God, I am nobody. If my image is not like the holy God, I am nothing.

When the nearsighted by unbelief glance at themselves in the mirror, they cannot see the hidden persons of their hearts. They look at their own goodness and feel good about themselves. They appear to be wise, powerful, and significant, and have a high opinion of themselves. They take pride in appearance. But are they as good as they appear?

When we measure ourselves by ourselves, we exalt ourselves highly and boast beyond our measure. We commend ourselves and view other sinners with contempt. We trust in ourselves that we are righteous. The true reality of a person can be found in the person of the heart past the appearance of personal image and behind the façade of reputations in the world. The appearance is deceiving. There are sinister secrets in our hearts. Who has no wounds, spots, or blemishes?

We do not know what we are truly, until we are assessed by the stature of Jesus, the Son of God. Unless we know Him, we do not know ourselves truly because He is the truth. When we measure ourselves against the true standard of God, we see what we are in truth. Therefore, we must turn to the true, perfect man Jesus. He is the image and the exact representation of God. He shows the true stature of what man must be like. He is the holy One. Jesus is the true measure of manhood. He believes in God the Father. While being crucified on the cross, He kept entrusting Himself to the Father and obeyed the Father's will. The true man did not live for His own life and glory. In the continuous fellowship with God the Father and the absolute dependence upon the Father, He devoted His life to His Father's glory. Jesus was a man of compassion. He had concerns for others, especially for the poor and afflicted. He helped the sick and oppressed. The perfect man mingled with the despised and loved even His enemies. In selflessness, He sacrificed Himself for poor sinners. Jesus committed no sin.

Jesus provides the true standard of man against which a person must be measured. The distance from the Son of God Jesus shows the true estimate of the person. If we fail to measure up to the fullness of Jesus, we fall short of being the perfect man. The ignorant of God are haughty in mind, but they do not know that they are wretched and miserable sinners.

Have you ever compared yourself with Jesus? If not, have a good look at the Son of God and take a truthful look at yourself. See how you measure up to the standard of God for man.

No Knowledge of Life

People search for the meaning of life by asking, "What is life? What does it mean to have life?"

When we are alienated from Jesus Christ and are excluded from the life of God, we do not know the meaning of life. Life is a mystery to the unbelievers. Consequently, life means different things to different people. If you ask ten people about the meaning of life, you will get ten different responses. In fact, people offer an infinite variety of meanings to life according to their personal views and experiments of life.

Human life has, by its nature, an eternal quality and therefore defies concise definition. It also has an eternal quantity and cannot be measured by worldly standards. Nevertheless, we always know when we have the life. We can see, enter, and experience it. The more we experience the life of God, the better we understand human life. Those who have personally experienced eternal life can describe what it is like.

The quality of life examines what kind of life a person has. It appraises whether life is good or bad. It asks the question whether a person is alive or dead.

When a person faces a near-death situation, medical professionals look for brain functioning, breathing, and heartbeat or pulse or both. When they sense the most basic body functions, they clinically consider the person is still alive. People say, "Look! I'm breathing. I can talk. I can walk. I'm still alive!" But they do not know that they do not have true life.

Look at plants in the field. They have life and breathe the air. As humans breathe the breath of life, so do the plants. If we have only the breath of life, we are no better than plants. A person who is still breathing through the nostrils but does not have the power of life to move, like immobile plants, bears the image of the plant. We know such a condition is more like a plant life. A person on a life-support system to remain in a vegetative state of life is called a "vegetable." The person does not have the power of life to move freely and is immobilized and bedridden. Then, there are the people we call "couch potatoes" or "computer potatoes," who are fixed on a couch in front of the television or immobilized before a computer. They love TV or the computer for life and look for the entertainment of life there. They are still breathing but have no power of action. They have no vitality to do the things they should do. Their lives are despondent. In addition, the one dwelling in one's own ivory tower does not have the freedom of movement. His or her dead heart is as hard as ivory and has no freedom to love neighbors, forgive others, or praise God.

Human life without the freedom of life is not really a life: it is an existence. The person deprived of the freedom of life remains alive with the breath of life and ekes out a bare existence from an immobilized living. Such a person neither see life nor know its meaning. It is not good that human beings should live like plants. A life lacking the vitality of life has no glory of human life. For a human being to have life means more than to have breath in the nostrils. Human life is much more than breath, just as human beings are much more than plants. Man is destined to a better life than the one for plants.

Most people have the movements of life—for example, eating, talking, and walking—but the unbelievers have no understanding, like unreasoning animals.

Observe how animals live. They have the power of life to move but do not have the knowledge of God, and live by natural instinct. People without understanding and wisdom live according to their natural desires, like animals. Those who move by natural instinct bear the image of animals. In fact, they are more like animals than humans.

Now, see the somatic moving creatures such as worms and bugs. Caterpillars do nothing else but eat food to fill their bodies with greed, but they never seem to be satisfied. They do not look up to the sky or sides for their neighbors.

There are people who do not look up to heaven or have thoughts about others but keep eating for life. They are more like worms and bugs. Money bugs love money and possessions. They devour money, cars, houses, and other properties but do not know the satisfaction of life. Bookworms have a great appetite for knowledge and keep eating books. They are always learning but never able to come to know the joy of life.

Some live like squirrels. They are always busy with the labor of collecting food for the future. Like a squirrel in a cage, they repeat the same routine of daily work. These people are too busy with running the rat race. They keep worrying about life and are anxious about tomorrow. They are insensitive about neighbors and have no fellowship of life with God or others. They do not know the rest and newness of life. Life to them is boredom and weariness.

Some live like the beasts of the field. They do not have the sense of good and evil, right and wrong, and honor and shame. They neither fear God nor respect others. People who live according to natural appetites bear the image of the beast. They have no self-control and live to gratify their carnal desires. They eat and drink to satisfy their own appetites, and touch for the pleasures of bodily excitement. Like beasts, their self-indulgence serves the flesh to satisfy their corrupt desires and degrading passions. They do improper and shameless deeds.

A husband is sometimes seen as a senseless beast in the eyes of his wife. Without an understanding and gentle heart, he does not care about his wife's needs and abuses her to satisfy his own desires like the beasts of the field. The story of *Beauty and the Beast* shows that man in his might, yet without understanding, is a beast.

When I married at my age of thirty-one, I knew nothing about marriage—namely, its purpose, objectives, and duties. I, an unbelieving and ignorant husband, knew neither the way of a happy marriage nor how to live with my wife in an understanding way. I did not understand the simple truth that my wife is a woman, and knew nothing about her spiritual needs. A pig will be satisfied with a full stomach, but a woman cannot live and prosper with only food, clothes, and shelter. When I did not nourish my wife with the word of life, she had no strength to build a home. She was not cherished with the faith and hope in Jesus Christ. She felt insecure in her own home without the love of her husband. Our marriage without love was meaningless. Because of my ignorance, I did not treat her with care and gentleness. Over the years, my wife was wounded by my unloving, critical words, and her heart was filled with sorrow and pain. She withered without blossoming when I neglected my duties to love her and supply her spiritual needs. And she stopped singing the songs of joy and happiness when I acted ignorantly. With the belief that I could build up a happy home with my professional career, I worked hard at my job. My heart was preoccupied with my work and my relationships with my wife were impersonal and intellectual. Contrary to my wishes for a happy marriage, the first three years of our marriage were wet and miserable like the winter weather in Vancouver. Our home was in ruins in spite of all my wishes and efforts. I could not build up a happy home with my ignorance.

We know that it is not good for humans to live like animals. People with an animal life do not understand the meaning of life because human life is more than animal life. Human beings have more dignity and honor than animals. For a person to have life is more than to have a beating heart, warm blood, and pulses in the body. Human life is more than moving with the power of life in the body. Man does not live by breathing and body movements alone.

Our Maker formed the man of dust from the ground and blew into his nostrils the breath of life (the spirit of life), and the man became a living soul. The Spirit of God gives life to the body of man. Human life is more than physical life, as the person of man is more than the body of man. It has a spiritual, eternal quality. The qualities of human life are righteousness, love, peace, joy, patience, kindness, faithfulness, gentleness, self-control, and the like. These qualities are the deep longing of human soul. People with these qualities bear the image of God. Human life has a divine, heavenly, eternal quality. The spiritual qualities give meaning to life. Life means love. Life with peace has meaning. Life without joy is meaningless.

The spiritual qualities are the true vital signs and evidences of human life. If these qualities are ours, we have life. These qualities displayed in human life are the splendor of life. Then, we see life. We know we have a good life.

Now, you know how to examine your life. If the qualities of life are evident in your soul, you know you have life. Your life has meaning. But if you lack the qualities of life in your daily living, you do not have life. You are dead and perishing. You are not okay because you experience death. You know that your days of living are meaningless. The days of your life seem futile. You do not see the meaning or purpose of life.

If you are not a believer in Jesus Christ, you do not have the Spirit of God in you. You do not have life; you will see death and adversity in your daily living.

The quantity of life measures how much life we have. It asks how rich our life is. People judge life according to the abundance of earthly possessions. But a person's life does not consist of the person's worldly wealth. True wealth is the riches of spiritual qualities in the person of the heart. God's life has eternal quantity. It is abounding with the eternal qualities of life. The life overflowing with love, peace, and joy is meaningful.

Truly, human life is eternal life. It is the life of eternal quality in eternal quantity. Human life means eternal life. To have life means to have eternal life. This is the true life of man. This life is in Jesus Christ, not in the things of the world.

Eternal life gives human life its value. Life is worth living for the life of God. Life without eternal life is worthless and useless. The life is also the reason to live. The life of God is the true lifestyle of man. Eternal life is the measure of life. If our lives come short of eternal life, we feel frustrated with our lives. No matter how rich we are in the things of the world, our lives without eternal life are lacking.

Speculating in the Darkened Heart

In the days of unbelief and ignorance, we can only speculate about all things in the darkness of our hearts. We cannot see the transcendent truth with our weakness of nearsightedness and blindness, so we speculate by the apparent reality of things. We judge by what our eyes see and make a decision by what our ears hear. Leaning on our own understanding and counsels, we conjecture with our imaginations and presumption.

The intellectuals of the world attempt to explain the questions of God, the world, man, and life with all branches of human sciences (e.g., theology, philosophy, science). But their speculations in darkness lead them to errors and they exchange the truth of God for the falsehood of man. Then, they raise up the lofty things of speculations at variance with the truth of God.

When the mystery of godliness is unknown, religious people speculate about godliness. They make their own gods and invent their religions. They organize belief systems about their deities according to the elementary principles of the world. Many speculations about godliness are evident in a wide variety of worldly religions. There are many beliefs and religions in the world.

Religions of human invention have the appearance of godliness. They consist of externals and are empty inside. People of worldly religions attain a form of godliness but not the power of godliness. They look righteous and stand tall outside but fall inside with heavy hearts burdened with sin and guilt. Even though they work hard for godliness with good intention and much effort, they fail to find life and see death in their souls.

Theology is a human way of acquiring the knowledge of God. Theologians study the Scriptures to know God by their own methodologies rather than according to Jesus Christ. Biblical scholars also take their intellectual approaches in pursuing the knowledge of God. So far, they have formulated many theologies and doctrines for Christianity, for example, Catholicism, Calvinism, Arminianism, and denominationalism. Many opinions and disagreements about God show that theological knowledge is partial, not one. (The Lord our God is one.) Theologies deal with human dogmas for religious beliefs and practices.

You come to the Bible to know God. If you do not fix your eyes on Jesus the Son of God witnessed by the Bible but study the letter of the Bible, you will come short of the knowledge of God.

Our faith in Jesus Christ rests not on the theological knowledge gained by human wisdom but on the full conviction brought by the Holy Spirit, the power of God. And we believe in our hearts that Jesus is the Christ, the Son of God. The heart understanding of God is different from the head knowledge of God. Obviously, we do not come to know God through the human knowledge of theology.

The world's religions speculate about divine worship according to the religious traditions and teachings of men. For instance, those who have never seen the presence of God build earthly sanctuaries (e.g., temples, churches, synagogues, mosques, shrines) as the house of God. And they prepare the earthly houses to look holy and dedicate them to God. But the God of heaven does not dwell in the buildings prepared by human hands with earthly things.

The clergy, priests, or ministers appointed by human agencies enter the earthly buildings and perform the divine worship according to men's traditions and regulations. The laity, or common people, come to the "sanctuary" for worship and prayers, and they serve God in their own ways.

When I was ignorant, I did not know how to pray, as I must pray by the Holy Spirit through Jesus Christ. Hearing about difficulty in the delivery of our first baby, Sharon, I felt the need of God's help for the first time in my life. Whenever I closed my eyes to pray, my eyes were filled with fluttering lights and pandemonium. My prayers wandered in the vast universe and perished into darkness.

All human religions presumptuously require people to work their ways up to God and enter heaven. Some religious leaders teach the lie that heaven is open to all, including those who do not believe in Jesus Christ, as long as they are good. Not knowing the righteousness of God in Jesus Christ, the leaders and followers work for their own righteousness with a sincere heart. Good works, however, cannot make them perfect in conscience. They know the evil conscience in their hearts.

Philosophy is a human way of pursuing the wisdom for life. The intellects of the age seek the knowledge of life in their minds. They indulge in introspection and conjectural thoughts and by far have speculated numerous schools and doctrines of philosophy and a variety of guides to life. They counsel the public by many confusing and controversial words. Friedrich Nietzsche could not find God in the minds and lives of Christians and said, "God is dead." He could not believe in God through his philosophical speculations in his brilliant mind. His philosophy misled my unstable soul. Soren Kierkegaard thought of marriage in the following way: "Whether you marry or you do not marry, you will regret it either way." His philosophy confused my young heart.

Philosophy begins with abstract thoughts in human mind and has no insight into spiritual realm or the natural world. The truth and wisdom of God cannot be found in human mind; they are not there. Philosophy is also based on subjective inquiries and speculations; therefore, philosophers are unable to come to know the truth of God through their human wisdom. The intellects without understanding fail to come to know God or His wisdom for eternal life through philosophy.

On the other hand, the scientists who are skeptical about both theological dogmas and philosophical thoughts pursue the truth in the natural world by scientific methods. Turned from the truth in Jesus Christ, they search for the truth and nature of the physical world. They study the physics, chemistry, biology, and geology of material things. They speculate on the truth by devising and testing of theses and hypotheses. By scientific methods, they observe natural phenomena of the world, collect data, and reason for their hypotheses. They judge by the appearance of things and formulate possible theses. Then, they do experiments and tests to establish scientific facts or evidences for their theories.

Unbelieving scientists seek the truth to explain scientifically the origin of the universe. Being ignorant of God's creation, they speculate along their scientific understanding and propose the big bang theory for the early development of the universe. They think the rudimentary notion that the universe was originated from physical things. They dismiss God's work of creation by saying, "The story of creation is a myth. It is a mere legend." God's word on the beginning of the world is beyond the reach of their minds, and they reject it. Without scientific evidences, they remain skeptical about everything, even the truth of God.

Physicists see the universe obeying certain laws but understand these laws only in part. There have been many discoveries and theories about the universe, but it still remains an unsolved mystery to them. Many things are not known about it. Up to now, the science about the material universe has led to quantum theory, the theory of relativity, M theory, and other theories. While maintaining their various theories with scientific evidences, physicists are involved in discussions about the knowledge of the universe.

Biologists speculate about the origin of species. Observing mutation and evolution in nature, they have formulated the theory of evolution for plants and animal species by scientific speculations. Nearsighted biologists see evolution with their eyes and deny the creation of God in a mystery. The theory of evolution is easier to understand with human mind, for evolution is scientifically visible. On the contrary, creation is invisible. When I was ignorant about the Lord God of heaven and earth, evolution was all I knew. Creation was too wonderful for me to understand.

The origin of man is also speculated by scientific theories. The theory of human evolution stipulates that plants and animals are precursors of man. Paleoanthropologists study fossils of ancient human-like animals and assume a human link. Observing the resemblance between humans and animals, they hold the theory that gorillas and chimpanzees are human ancestors. Many scientists maintain that man is not a creation of God but a natural product, though they cannot tell which came first: man or woman, chicken or eggs. The creatures say to their Creator, "You did not make us. We are from animals."

The truth of God transcends empirically discovered theories. It is invisible and beyond the sights of unbelieving scientists and cannot be discovered by them through their own efforts. Science speaks the power of nature, not the wonders of God. Creation is beyond human reason and natural power. The miracle of God is unintelligible and incredible for rational explanations. Creation is not the thing that scientists have ever seen or understood, and it defies all human reasoning and science. Creation means what is seen was not made out of the visible things of nature. It deals with the supernatural power of God's word. It is sudden, radical changes by the power of God in the twinkling of an eye. When God said, "Let there be light," immediately there was light.

Scientists do great—sometimes, wonderful—works to help us to understand the natural world. We should, however, consider the weaknesses of science. First, scientific knowledge is nearsighted and partial because science focuses on the physical world only. Science is unable to recognize the supernatural world. Hence, it falls short of spiritual truth. It cannot explain miracles—the wonders of God. It is a miracle for an unbeliever like me to become a believer in Jesus Christ. The miracle of miracles is that a sinner like me became a saint by the wonderful works of God. The things lying beyond the reach of scientific investigations remain in a mystery. Second, scientific knowledge changes as the nature of seen things does. The natural phenomena observed by science are temporal and changing. Third, scientific knowledge is limited because scientific methods and observations are prone to human limitations.

The ignorant of the truth of God also have to speculate about the ways of life in the world. They judge life by sight and make decisions about life choices in ignorance. Such important decisions as career and marriage are made by speculations.

Not knowing the way of God to eternal life, I speculated about my career to life. At the age of thirteen when I lifted my eyes to the mountains, they called me to come to them for life. The beauty of trees and forests was pleasing to my sight and my heart. I loved the mountains so much that I wanted to live in them. Consequently, forestry became a major subject in my university education. Without any knowledge about the careers in the world, I sought a career as a professor and researcher in forestry.

When I came to Vancouver, Canada as a landed immigrant, I saw the beautiful mountains and forests and the prosperous forest products industries in the province of British Columbia. Now a career in forest products technology appeared promising. So I turned to a career in the pulp and paper technology.

After seven years of working in the pulp and paper industry, I wanted a change because I could not find the path of peace and joy there. For quick and easy money, I set my sights on the booming real estate market in Vancouver. The farmland with the potential of housing development became my gaze. I managed a mushroom farm and then a landscaping business.

To find a career to life, I often changed my occupations and tried new careers. Again and again I embarked on the endeavors that seemed to promise life, but I could not find life in my careers in the world.

How do we choose our marriage partners? Most of us choose a particular individual by speculations according to our eyes and ears. Many men pick their spouses by external attractiveness or visual stimulus. If a woman looks good and right in the eyes of a man, he desires her as his wife. On the other hand, many women judge men by their financial and social status. They choose their men by what they hear about occupations in the world. And they prefer doctors/dentists, judges/lawyers, or engineers to poor men with the invisible quality of a gentle and loving spirit. They value financial security more than personal quality.

When I started my courtship of a vivacious woman, Grace, I sent a letter with her photographs to introduce her to my parents in Korea. They did not ask about the person of her heart, and they flatly opposed my marriage to her. The sole reason was that she is a Christian. They alleged that Christians honor God, not ancestors. After the letter, there was no more communications from them. We married without their approval in June 1973.

When we face an important and difficult decision, we agonize over it. Even after making a decision, we are not sure whether we made the right decision or not. Doubts linger over a chosen career, a marriage partner, and other decisions. Our decisions by speculations are unsettled; our hearts are churning.

In the timid days of my youth when I did not have the faith in Jesus Christ, purchasing big items was challenging to me. I had to judge major purchases not with true judgment but by speculations. My doubting heart was troubled even after the purchase. Nothing was stable to me, an ignorant and speculating man.

The Misguided and Separated

The Misguided by the World

The world calls the unbelieving and ignorant, "Come to me, and I will give you life. I will make you rich. I will make your name great." The god of this world tempts the naive souls to believe the lie.

Simple ones readily respond to the call of the world and turn their eyes to the world. As they behold the glory of the world, their eyes are opened by the light of the world's glory and see the glamour of money, the splendor of fame, the power of position, and the pleasures in the world. A dream house is a delight to their hearts. A brand-new car in a show room is good for a ride in style. Good-looking men and women attract their eyes.

The beholders of the glory of the world become blind, just as the bright light of the sun blinds the eyes of the gazer. Their hearts in blinding darkness are unable to see the truth about the world. The god of this world entices unstable souls to come to the world and love and worship the things in the world for life and glory. The ones blinded by infatuation lust after their lovers without understanding.

The glory of the world is deceptive. The world once deceived my heart into believing its false promise. Enticed by the lust of my eyes, I fell in love with the world and desired the world for my life and glory. I fixed my hope completely on the life and glory in the world that will be mine. When I followed my heart, I went astray from the right way of God to the world. Thus, I entered the world.

Once we enter the world, it misguides us to make our own gods of creatures for ourselves and set up idols in our hearts. Man-made gods are by nature not gods at all; they are idols, non-existent things. A god or an idol is the person or the thing that a person loves and worships for life. The error of idolatry is to love and worship creatures rather than God the Creator. (To worship is to offer up the eyes, heart, and body as a sacrifice.)

In the hope of life and glory, each one goes after one's chosen god. The nations in the world seek their own gods. Lovers of wealth pursue the god of money. Unprincipled politicians love the god of power more than the people of the land. Lovers of position climb up the ladder of hierarchy. Lovers of pleasure walk after the god of sex.

What is your idol? You do not have to set up a graven image or object in your house or shrine. You set up your idol in the shrine of your heart. Your darling, hero, career, house, or car fills your heart and overcomes you. You love and serve your idol with all of your soul and body. Your idol makes you estranged from God, becomes the snare of evil to you, and makes you to sin.

The idols of this age are money, fame, and sex. People want to get rich and famous. Their hearts are preoccupied with material possessions; there is no room for the eternal things of God. They trust in the riches of the world rather than in God. Many business people love wealth on earth more than the riches in heaven.

People know well the names of the heroes of the world but do not recognize the names of the heroes of faith in the Bible. They love and worship their stars and heroes, and enthusiastically admire celebrities—namely, actors, singers, and athletes. Musicians esteem Beethoven, Mozart, and Bach. Computer lovers adore Bill Gates and Steve Jobs. It appears to them that the most famous, successful individuals will show the way to life and glory.

Nevertheless, we do not understand the strange gods in the world such as money, fame, position, and pleasures. About money, for example, we do not know its peril at all. Nor do we know the deceptiveness of worldly riches. God warns us: "People who want to get rich fall into temptation and a trap and into many foolish and harmful desires that plunge men into ruin and destruction. For the love of money is a root of all kinds of evil." The purpose of money is not to accumulate it and get wealthy for us but to use it for the good of others. We are not the owners of money but its stewards. Good stewards share riches with the poor.

The gods in the world are uncertain; they are vanity. They cannot save us from our troubles or give us eternal life. Yet we placed our faith and hope in them.

Besides, we do not even know the true desire of our souls. We have no concerns for the things of God for our souls and care for only the things on earth for our bodies.

The Deceived by Sin

The bait promises life to a fish. It looks good for food to the eyes of the fish. Deceived by its alluring appearance, the fish desires it. The fish is carried away, goes after, and swallows the baited hook. Then the fish is caught by the hook. Like fish hooked by allurement and animals trapped in snares, men and women are deceived by sin.

Sin deceives senseless people with the promise of life. If something looks good in their eyes, they are tempted by sin. When the lust of their eyes overwhelms them to gaze at the bait, they are carried away by their desire and go after it. They are hooked when they swallow it. They fall into sin and commit sin. When David, a king of Israel, saw a woman bathing, the woman was very beautiful in his eyes. He looked with desire at his neighbor's wife and was tempted by his own lust. So he took Bathsheba for himself and committed the sin of adultery.

Sin has a blinding power. Once sin fills our hearts, we are no longer able to see anything. The darkness of sin blinds the eyes of the sinner. Anger blinds the eyes of the angry person. The man who looks on a woman to lust after her is in darkness; the eyes full of adultery cannot see. The bribe blinds the sighted on materials and distorts justice in the dark. Those who view others with haughty eyes become blind and despise them.

Sin seduces the ignorant. The adulteress seduces a man thirsty for love with flattering lips by saying, "Come and drink love from me, and you will be satisfied." If he follows her, the strange woman will catch the foolish man in a snare.

The deceitfulness of sin enticed me to sell my soul. The pleasures in the world appeared to me to be good for my life. My foolish heart desired many harmful and shameful things. I followed the lusts of my heart for the pleasures of sin and spent my life in ungodliness and unrighteousness.

Satan, the tempter, lures the innocent into sin through his seductive deception. He lays a snare for the ignorant. He misleads the unbelieving and ignorant to disobey the word of God. They are deceived and seek after their own hearts to sin, as Satan deceived Eve by his craftiness. When the serpent, Satan, tempted Eve with misleading words, she listened to his false words and looked at the tree in the garden in Eden. She saw that "the fruit of the tree was good for food and pleasing to the eye, and also desirable for gaining wisdom." Beholding the beauty of the fruit of the tree, Eve could not see the word of God about the fruit. Her soul without understanding was secretly deceived by Satan. She followed her eyes, was carried away, and was enticed by her own desire. Her heart desired to have the fruit. And she went after the tree, took the forbidden fruit, and ate it in disobedience. Adam and Eve despised the word of God by the deceitfulness of sin.

Our hearts misguided by the world and deceived by sin forsake the way of God in Jesus Christ and turn to the way of man in the world. And we seek our own life and glory, not God's.

The Separated from God

Apostasy and idolatry make a separation between God and the unbelievers. Sin leads them from God to walk the evil ways in the world, far from God. A person without God is alienated from the God of life. The person is an alien and stranger to God.

Do you see how far you are away from God? If you feel a great chasm from God, you are separated from God and stand alone in the world.

Lovers of the world are enemies of God. The enmity in their hearts is the barrier of the dividing wall between God and the unbelievers. They are unable to cross over to come to God; there is an abyss of darkness separating God and them.

The Exiled from the Life of God

Those who are alienated from God are excluded from His life. Sin carries them away into exile to the world. The exiles live an evil life in a distant land that is not their homeland. Adam and Eve disobeyed the word of God and were driven out of the good life in the Garden of Eden to the life of adversity and death in the world. Eve brought forth children in great pain and Adam toiled for food until they returned to dust. Israelites in the Bible sinned against God and were exiled from the Promised Land of Canaan to foreign lands of slavery and sufferings, far away from their homeland. The unbelievers, being exiled far from the life of God, are left to themselves in the strange land of this world. They strive with their own resources for the life in the world.

2. Man's Works in the World

The Toils of Occupation
The Needs for the Body
The Occupation for Bodily Needs

The Labors for Sin
The Desires of the Flesh
The Labors for Sin

The Works for Godliness and Righteousness
The Wishes of the Soul
The Works of the Laws
The Works for Personal Development

Now, what do we strive for in the world?

To succeed in the world, we plan our own ways to gain the world. We make every effort to obtain the good things of the world—namely, long life, wealth, position, honor, and pleasures. In our quest for a happy life in the world, many of us do our utmost with the ambitions of the world.

In this chapter, man's works in the world include the toils of occupation, the labors for sin, and the works for godliness and righteousness.

The Toils of Occupation

The Needs for the Body

The body of man came from earth and needs earthly things for its life, whereas the soul of man came from God and needs the things of God for its life. Our God counsels not to worry about earthly things but to seek first the things of God for life. The reasons are as follows: First, man does not live by earthly goods alone. Second, God provides all things for life in His grace to those who believe in Him. Therefore, man's vocation is to do the work of God—that is, to believe in the Lord Jesus.

Nevertheless, the unbelievers spurn the counsel of God and say in their hearts, "Will God supply all my needs? No, He will not. I will believe in myself and serve the world for my life." They think that the world will supply all their needs for life and glory. Their unbelieving hearts are anxious for their lives about what to eat, and for their bodies about what to put on and where to dwell. The unbelievers strive to make their own provision for their bodies in the fear of poverty, sickness, and death. Their priority is earthly things over heavenly things: they seek first the things that are on earth. In fact, their minds are so preoccupied with earthly things that they have no concern for the heavenly things of God for their souls. Ungodly Esau, a son of the Hebrew patriarch Isaac, sold his birthright for some bread and some lentil stew. His mind was obsessed with his immediate need of food for his body, and he despised the rich promises of God. He sought rather to fill his stomach for the strength of his body than to obtain the privilege of God's blessings. We too lived for our bodies; our lives were spent for eating, drinking, clothing, and housing.

The Occupation for Bodily Needs

The care for our bodies inspires us to work for earthly things.

Everyone seeks an occupation to earn a livelihood. We earn a living by our works with our knowledge and strength. Our knowledge is the skills for professions or trades. Our strength is the body of earth.

Each of us tries to find a career. (A career is a course of occupation.) Each turns to a chosen course of trade or profession. Once a career is set, each pursues it by following a career path. For our careers, we look for a good education, increase our occupational skills, and search for a better job or business.

We the ambitious people look for plentiful harvest from the world and devote ourselves to our works. We rise up early, go to work, and retire late. Workaholics among us do not even rest at home or at night, tossing until dawn. We are in the rat race and climb the ladder of success. Sometimes we get caught up in stressful routines and busyness. When the task is too great for us, we burn out our lives with zeal and labor.

The glory of wealth makes us strive after money to live well in a stylish house in an upscale community. We desire luxurious living in a larger house filled with earthly goods. With covetousness we seek extravagance for the purpose of displaying personal vanity and self-vaunting opulence. Our greedy hearts want more and more. We increase houses and multiply properties. We accumulate earthly goods beyond our own needs and store up in storehouses for many years to come. Wealthy people living in a mansion or a penthouse suite cannot stay in their homes with contentment and leave them to seek the satisfaction of life somewhere else.

For success in the world, I started with lofty ambition. My vision was to reach up to the stars of the sky. I dreamed that my power and glory would govern the Pacific Rim. To see the vision, at the age of seventeen I left my parents' house in a village and came to the world of a larger city. I hoped that I would see my glory and have a happy life through my works in the world.

Most of the years of my youth were spent in finding a career in the world. At school, I studied hard with determination and sacrifices. With eagerness I rose early in the morning and stayed up late in the evening. When my career in forestry was set, I pursued it with energetic fervor and ardent efforts. To prepare for the entrance examination for a prestigious university, I took extracurricular studies in the evenings after my regular school programs. The rooms for the evening classes were so cold in winter nights that I had to warm my numb hands and frozen fountain pen slipping on the paper by blowing my breath. I missed the many fun things that young people do. To me, my career was my life; I could suffer hardships and sacrifices.

After university education and compulsory military service, I undertook teaching and researching in the field of silviculture. With the hope of life, I endured the toils of performing long hours of scientific experiments and reading many professional books and journals. But I could not find the work for life in Korea.

So I moved on to Vancouver, Canada at my age of twenty-eight for a new and better life. I looked around to find a way to life in the foreign city. Soon, desiring to study further, I embarked on a Master of Science program in the wood and pulp science at the University of British Columbia. It was formidable for me to take a new course in the strange land of foreign language and culture. For my researches, I was exposed to toxic chemical fumes and harmful X-ray and gamma ray.

In my cleverness I devised my plan to succeed in the new world of Canada. I first sought after my professional career in teaching and researching at a university. But when I was completing my MS program, my true bent came to the fore. My love was not the study on a university campus but money and fame in the world. I was so anxious to pursue my lovers in the world that I could not see myself doing another four or five years' study for a PhD degree. Hence, I did not pursue the academic degree and ran to the world.

I often changed my occupations and careers to discover the work for life. But I could not find it in the world. There were only toils and problems in all the careers that I took. For my job at a consulting company for the pulp and paper industry, I struggled with high-pressure steam and corrosive chemicals at a pilot plant. I wiped away the streaming sweat on my body as I travailed in labor for a living. Then I studied business management and engaged in business ventures to enlarge my works in the world. One summer when I labored with pyramidal cedars at a tree farm, the sweltering heat on the open field beat on my exhausted body and I became weary. In a mushroom farm where I had difficulty with a spawning machine, my body was burdened excessively, beyond my strength. I lay on a sick bed for a few days. Then being occupied with the landscaping business, I ran all over Greater Vancouver from my office to job sites and nurseries. When real estate development slowed down, I stopped. God knows my toils and affliction in the world.

The prodigious labors took their tolls on me. My desires for the world left me in the dangers of death many times. My burning zeal for success in the world consumed me and I became like ashes.

By my toils of occupations, I succeeded in gaining earthly things. I ate the produce of earth, put on clothes, and dwelled in houses. But

I could not satisfy my insatiable appetite for possessions. I made my living but failed to have life. I tried various careers in the world but could not find a path to life there. I sought for life with my wisdom of the world but could not see peace for my soul. I wrested a living from the world but could not enter life. I ate the fruit of my labor to fill my belly, but my life was not satisfied. I spent my earnings for clothing, but my heart was not warm enough. I prepared houses for my body, but there was no place for me to dwell in peace and glory. From all my works in the world, I could not attain the newness of life. I was bored by the routine tasks of everyday life. My soul did not know peace and rest in my works and was burdened with fatigue and weariness. The worries of life over many things and the cares for the needs of daily life weighed down my heart. I struggled with the strength of my body, frail and weak as it was through the body of dust. Daily hassles wore me out to dust. The pressures of my jobs burdened stress on me. My works in the world became a burden instead of a blessing, and toil instead of joy. My occupation was a grim duty.

The Labors for Sin

The Desires of the Flesh

The flesh of man has its desires, including evil ones. People of the flesh set their minds on the things of the flesh. The lusts of the flesh are too powerful and irresistible for the unbelievers, who rely on the weakness of the flesh. (Lust is intense desire for self-gratification.) They feel that they would die if they do not serve fleshly lusts. So the natural men and women are under obligation to fleshly lusts. To satisfy the lusts, they make provision for the flesh in its lusts and pleasures. In the hope of life and fleshly pleasures, they work hard to satisfy the evil desires of the flesh. They carry out the deceitful desires, against their wishes, and eat, drink, and touch for the delights of the flesh. Thus they are very busy with the labors for sin.

The Labors for Sin

It is normal for a healthy person to have an appetite for food. Eating food for the care of the body is a good work. But the flesh wants to eat food for the satisfaction of life. People of the flesh try to fill the emptiness of life with food and cater to their lustful appetite. Eating with lust and indulgence in the love of food is gluttony.

The desire for sex is natural. The acts of sex within a marriage are sanctified by God to meet the spouse's sexual needs. The husband and wife have the holy duty to each other. When we turn away from the way of God for human sexuality, however, we walk downward to sexual immorality. Our flesh craves after sex beyond the will of God. Having eyes full of lust, we burn our bodies with immoral passion. We give our bodies to degrading passions for the practices of sensuality and impurity. We exploit our bodies to serve our own cravings. If we desire our spouses for our own gratification, the passion degrades us to animals. Adulterers and adulteresses seek the satisfaction of life in sex out of marriage. Adultery is a perversion of the intimacy of married love. After having many women (seven hundred wives and three hundred concubines) and stimulating his body with frenzies of pleasures, Solomon, a king of Israel, found that his labors for the flesh were vanity.

The Bible says that homosexuality is a perversion of the natural functions of men and women. The contemporary perversions are not new. The men of Sodom and Gomorrah in the ancient times indulged in the unnatural lust and indecent acts.

The flesh desires to possess materials for the riches of life. The lust for possession is avarice. We wanted to gain more than we needed to satisfy our lust for wealth. With cupidity we accumulated materials. Ahab, a king of Israel, wished to extend his extravagance and indulgence in luxury by acquiring his neighbor's vineyard. The king murdered Naboth, his neighbor, and took possession of his vineyard.

Sin satisfies the sinner because it satisfies the lusts of the flesh. Sinners labor for passing pleasures and find temporal satisfaction in sin. With sinning, they make their hearts glad; they count fleshly pleasures as the happiness of life. Sin is pleasure to the sinners, for sin is delight to the flesh. But sin is bitter to the soul, "for the wages of sin is death."

We loved fleshly pleasures and indulged our flesh in its insatiable desires. We did the works of the flesh, which include drunkenness, sexual immorality, envy, jealousy, and the like. Thus, we kept sinning and still asked for more.

Sin abounds in the lives of people in the flesh. We are murderers, adulterers, and robbers. When we are angry with our neighbors without cause, we are guilty of murder to go into the fiery hell. Adultery is already committed in our hearts when we look on a woman or a man in the sexual lust. If we do not share our possessions with the poor, we rob our neighbors.

At the youthful age of twenty-six, I had two jobs in Seoul, Korea. My daytime job was for my body and I labored for my flesh in the night. The great city was a perfect place for me, a prodigal man with freedom and money. When my flesh called me to its pleasures, my heart was wide-open for the call. I followed my heart and none could restrain my drive. The whirlwind of excitement rushed me to the downtown or the east side of Seoul. In the darkness of the night, I pursued fleshly delights such as parties, drunkenness, songs, dance, and laughter. I enjoyed the works of the flesh so much that I could not foresee what benefits I would receive for my labors. Later I came to know the pain of death.

I, a clever man yet without understanding, was foolish enough to be deceived by the pleasures of the flesh. It was out of curiosity that I wanted to stimulate my flesh with pleasures. At first, with uneasiness I tested my flesh with a small dose of alcohol and dance. Experiencing all the delights of my bodily senses, I loved the carnal pleasures. Then I worked hard to satisfy my fleshly lusts and engaged in shameful and embarrassing deeds. When I labored on the slippery ways of fleshly lusts and pleasures, I fell into the bog of sin.

The Works for Godliness and Righteousness

The Wishes of the Soul

The soul of man wishes godliness and righteousness. These are the deepest desire of human soul. Man has God-ward desire and wants to be holy and perfect. We long for righteousness and holiness. In the midst of our works for bodily needs and fleshly lusts, we make efforts to rise above the life of ungodliness and unrighteousness.

Godliness is the goal of man. To reach the goal, man strives for God-like qualities. The unbelievers pursue godliness and righteousness not by faith in Jesus Christ but by their own works. They work to develop godly characters and to attain the perfection of God.

The Works of the Laws

People of worldly religions do not know the godliness and righteousness revealed through Jesus Christ. So they work the laws—God's laws or man-made laws or both—to attain the righteousness in the laws. They think they can earn the salvation of God as a deserved reward for their works of the laws. They do their best to do good by their own efforts to please God. Then they claim on God's favor for their good works.

The people entrusted with the law of God know that the Law is righteous. They fix their hope on the Law and pursue the righteousness of God in the Law for themselves. Many meticulously observe the letter of the Law. Some strive under the Law to go beyond its literal requirements to be holy and blameless. They think their achievements deserve the favor of God. They believe that they are the ones who will get into the kingdom of God. Having their own righteousness in the Law, they trust in themselves that they are righteous. The self-righteous have confidence in their achievements rather than in the grace of God in Jesus Christ. They do not see the righteousness of God revealed by faith but look at their good works of the Law.

God-fearers who do not have the law of God work the things of the Law according to the teachings of people. They delight in their religious traditions. They imagine that they are capable of achieving righteousness through their own efforts. They consider themselves righteous and do not see themselves as sinners. They justify themselves before God and man and reject the Savior of the world, Jesus.

The workers of the laws stand tall before others, for they look godly outwardly. They justify themselves in the sight of men, but God knows their hearts. They do not have the power of godliness and hold to a form of godliness. They practice their righteousness before people to be honored by them. But God searches the heart for His righteousness. Their hearts are heavy-laden with the burdens of sin and guilt. Their lives are hollow and unreal. They know they are not perfect and do not have confidence to enter the holy presence of God. Then they learn that they need the Savior God.

The Works for Personal Development

Man's soul desires to be perfect, as God the Maker is perfect. (We all are perfectionists by nature.) We should be holy, as our God is holy. We need holiness and perfection, and our desire is to grow up to the stature of God. We pursue moral virtues and ethical excellence, and endeavor to be in all our glory without stains or spots or any other blemish.

When we do not know that we are of dust and weakness, we imagine that we are capable of attaining the perfect man and life through our own works. We seek perfection through personal development and strive to establish ourselves by our own efforts.

In the faith that I can perfect myself by my own efforts, I pursued perfection in my heart, mind, and body. To become a man of moral perfection, I took personal development courses on ethics and morality. For the wisdom and power of life, I read many books on life. For my physical perfection, I did all sorts of physical exercises and martial arts, including a black belt in *tae kwon do* (a Korean martial art).

Although I saw some progressive development in becoming a better person over the years through some renovations and alterations, the changes were partial and incomplete. I could not see a transformed heart or new life for me. I grew older with years but remained as the same old man of immaturity and timidity until I became a Christian. Contrary to my wishes and efforts, endless books for personal development left me in confusion and weariness. None of books and educational courses gave me the power of God to do the things that my spirit wished. Consequently, I repeated my folly in my weakness.

Part Two: The Life in the World

When we are exiled from the life of God in Jesus Christ and work for the life in the world, we are in manifold troubles. We serve our enemies in captivity and in poverty until we die, become like a desert, and perish in hell.

The following three chapters describe the life in the world. Three life conditions in the world—captivity, poverty, and wilderness—are chosen and separately focused on for the sake of clearer description.

3. Captivity

Subjection to the Elements of the World

Servitude to the Things on Earth
Money
Gambling
Technology
Hobbies
Tobacco
Alcohol
Drugs

Slavery to Sin in the Flesh
The Slaves of Sin
Spending Life in Sins
The Dead in Sin

We love freedom. Our careless hearts desire to be free even from the Lord our God. When we do not know the Lord God, we are the lords (masters) of our lives. We want unrestrained enjoyment of freedom in the world. Our wayward hearts say, "I am free to roam in the world. I can do anything as I please. I will live my life as I wish. I will use my body as I want."

The freedom from the Lord God is false freedom: it is freedom to be in captivity. As runaway sons and daughters from their parents are captured by the evil powers of the world, our freedom in the world results in bondage to the powers of the world. We use our freedom for the lusts of the flesh. And we are not as free as we think. We might be free from political or social bondage and think ourselves free. But when we are independent from God and exercise our freedom in the world, we are overcome by the powers of the world, taken captives, exiled from the life of God, and subjected to forced labors. This is our lives of oppression and struggle in the world. If we do not serve the Lord our God with love and joy, we will serve the powers of the world in humility and misery. The powers of the world have no respect for us and do not show us favor. The taskmasters in the world impose hard labors on us. We are oppressed and abused until we are destroyed under harsh servitude.

Those who have no God in their hearts are held in captivity by external and internal powers.

Subjection to the Elements of the World

The elements (*stoicheia* in Greek) of the world keep human souls in subjection. They are laws, conventions, traditions, theology, philosophy, science, and other elementary principles and teachings. The unbelievers, who are free from the Lord God, are held in captivity to the elemental forces.

Many people of Judaism, Christianity, and Islam are under the laws of God, the elementary teachings bound up with the world. They serve God in fear according to the letter of the laws as though God's righteousness and life were attained by the works of the laws. The laws control their lives. The religious people also place themselves under the rudimentary rules and regulations imposed by men and subject to dogmatic belief systems, traditions, and decrees.

The peoples of the nations in the world deify the elements of the world as gods and worship them. Among the objects of their worship are the heavenly luminaries (e.g., the sun, the moon, the stars), mountains, humans, animals, trees, and so forth. The elements of the world are the principalities and powers of the world; they are the rulers and authorities of this age. Peoples put themselves under the bondage of the elemental powers and submit to them in fear.

People without the truth of God are subject to theology, philosophy, and science, which are according to the elementary principles of the world and not according to Jesus Christ.

Besides, superstitions hold people in servitude. Superstitious beliefs about numbers and animals control their lives. Westerners are affected by a fear of Friday 13. The number 13 is an unlucky one and Friday is a day of bad luck to them. Many high-rise buildings in North America do not have a 13th floor. Chinese practice *Feng Shui* (a system using the principles of the sky and the earth for auspiciousness) and take the number 8 as good luck. Koreans and Japanese are superstitious about the number 4 phonetically sounding like the Chinese character for death. In Korea, ravens or crows mean bad omens and magpies mean good news.

Servitude to the Things on Earth

We humans are to be masters over the world and all things in it because the Lord God appointed us over His works. We are to have dominion over the world and rule all things on earth.

Nevertheless, if we love not the Lord our God but the things on earth for ourselves, we are possessed by their powers. Our lovers make us captives; they become our masters and control our lives. We let them reign over us and serve our lovers in servitude.

Money

Promising riches and financial freedom, money entices people of the world to love and worship it. Once their hearts are filled with the love of money, money occupies them and they become its captives. Now they are captured by the power of money and bound by the chains of money. The bondage is beyond their power to overcome. Money is their master; it rules over them. The captives of money serve money in bondage.

We hoped for financial freedom, but we were in financial captivity. We were preoccupied by money. We the captives of money were forced to serve it in avarice and covetousness. We obeyed whatever money commanded us to do. We did all sorts of evil to gain money: cheating, stealing, and robbing. The desire to get rich led us to ruins and pains.

Our houses and cars held us in servitude and imposed hard labor on us. Under the burdens of mortgages and loans, we spent our lives in serving them. When we were afflicted with servitude to our houses, we wondered who the master is—the house or the owner. Are our houses for us, or are we for our houses?

When I was young, I sought worldly possessions for the riches of life. But I could not find my path to the riches of life. I pursued money but could not overtake it. Rather I fell into temptation and snares. I was overcome and captured by money. As a captive of money, I was forced to do the evil things that I did not please. When the tyranny of money forced me to tell a falsehood in dishonesty for my gain, I lied. Later I groaned under the burdens of guilt.

Gambling

Some people love the thrill of gambling and enjoy it for a little while without a problem. Then, they dream of winning big money and start to go to gambling places more frequently. Soon gambling grabs hold of them and they quickly become captives of gambling. They obey its seductive lure and become regular servants to gambling. Once they get in there, they cannot get out. They are enslaved and become problem gamblers.

Problem gamblers try to resist the urge of gambling. But they have no control on their behavior. Being preoccupied with gambling, they cannot quit a gambling addiction. Those who are in the grip of gambling are unable to stay away from casinos, racetracks, lotteries, and other gambling places. When they do not find a solution, the downward spiral in their lives becomes helplessly accelerated. Gambling addicts lose everything, including money, job, friends, spouse, family, and houses. Then they touch bottom when the addiction consumes their lives. They become restless and desperate. Gambling destroys their characters and their lives.

Technology

Technology provides convenient communication, great entertainment, and much information for us. When we love and serve them for life, however, they will hold us in captivity.

If, for example, we love television, we become its slaves and have no power to turn it off; we serve it by watching it continuously. We hope for the rest and satisfaction of life from the screen, but we become more tired and feel empty.

Television was once my lover. I looked for the renewal of life from the TV and devoted my service of watching it for at least three hours a day. Looking for the TV to provide satisfying leisure, I was ready to vet and the TV was always there to oblige. But I ended up feeling invigorated later on. I tuned into one program after another until my exhausted body crawled to bed. The TV lulled me into lethargy and sloth. I felt fogged in and was in a rut.

While computers and electronic gadgets provide wonderful services for us, there are those who have become their captives. They seek life in there and dedicate so much time to them. Once captured on the Internet, it is difficult to give it up. They have trouble using it sensibly. The technological powers chain them to their computers and electronic devices. They spend their lives browsing the web; playing movies, games, and music; social networking, messaging, and sharing pictures and videos; and chatting, enjoying pornography, and spreading evil.

Hobbies

Once I was a captive of my hobbies: billiard, tennis, and golf. Whenever I was called out to my hobbies, I could not refuse. I obeyed and served them for my life. In return, they gave me dissatisfaction and frustration.

Tobacco

When I started smoking at nineteen, it was an unpleasant and painful experience. It left a bitter taste in my mouth. The smoke choked my throat and brought painful tears from my eyes. I had headaches. My body did not like it at all. Yet the fool endured all to serve tobacco.

Somehow in the midst of smoke and pain, I learned to taste its sensation. Soon I was captured by the bad habit and became addicted to smoking one- or two-pack-a-day. Whenever and wherever my body was urged to smoke, the captive had no power to refuse the urge and obeyed the craving. I, an honorable man to the eyes of people, was reduced to going down to the garage to find cigarette butts in the trashcan of my car.

Yes, I knew the health hazards of smoking, but still I continued to serve the harmful habit. Its hold on me grew stronger and more demanding. I puffed cigarettes like a smoking chimney and filled my body with smoke. The nasty, obnoxious, vile smell fouled my mouth. Smoking made my body stink and my teeth stained.

Every New Year's Day I resolved to break myself away from the grip of the bondage, but it was too strong for me. I struggled to quit the habit with resolutions and pledges, yet I did not have the power to butt out for good.

Alcohol

We start with social drinking. Our desires are to stimulate our bodies with alcohol and to make our hearts merry. We look for the joy of life in the bottom of the bottle. Some drink for courage. Others drink to forget their lives of burdens and pains.

"Drink me, and you will be satisfied." The alcohol deceitfully entices us. We want to drink more and more to be filled. Once our bodies are filled with the liquor, we are under the power of the substance. Alcohol takes control over the drunken. It forces the drunkard to do improper and indecent things.

Alcohol once betrayed and mocked me. When alcohol filled my body, its control went out of my way. I sang loudly and danced alone on the night streets of Seoul, reeling back and forth, finally embracing electrical poles on the sidewalks to keep me from falling. Like "a dog returning to its own vomit," I repeated my folly even after many vows and resolutions saying, "I will never do this again."

Some become alcoholics. Being shackled by the substance, alcoholics are not able to put the bottle down, and it ruins their lives. Their bodies are intoxicated and wasted by alcohol. They drink themselves to death and ruin.

Drugs

People try drugs and experiment with their bodies. They inhale and inject their choices of drugs for ecstasy. They smoke marijuana, snort cocaine, and hit the hard stuff like hallucinogens and newer drugs. When every cell in the body is filled with a tingling sensation, they feel euphoria. They get a taste for the drug and social use becomes a habit.

Regular users are addicted to drugs and dependent on them physically or psychologically or both. The addiction rules their lives; the addicts are not able to live freely. Now the captives of drugs have no freedom to say no to them. Every time they try to break the addiction's iron grip, they feel pain like kicking at a concrete wall with a bare foot. The draw to the drugs is just too much for them.

Before long, the addicted spend all their cash on drugs. They drift from friends, lose their housing, and begin living on the street. They work on the filthy streets. The runaway teenagers stroll looking for their next fix. Their lives suffer from the pains of prostitution, crime, and violence. They get into trouble.

Eventually, drug addicts are brought very low. Looking at themselves in the mirror is a painful experience. They hit rock bottom when everything they do revolves around drugs. Sooner or later, the drug kills the addicts.

Slavery to Sin in the Flesh

The Slaves of Sin

The flesh of man is indwelled by sin. Sin in the flesh desires the person, but he or she must master it. The unbelievers who make the flesh their strength, however, have no power to stand up before sin. They have no authority to say no to sin. Born of the flesh, they are weak through the flesh of earth. They are earthy and are as weak as dirt. Like clay before water, they are powerless and helpless before sin. Those of the flesh are defeated and captured by the enemy.

The law of God says, "Love your God and your neighbors." God gave us His law so that our lives go well with us. The Law is not rules and regulations, which we break if we can, but the wisdom for life and peace. The Law was given for our own good, just like the laws on using highways.

The signals, signs, and lines on the roads tell us the commandments of do's and don'ts. Where a maximum speed is posted, we should keep the speed. The red signal commands us, "Do not proceed but stop." We should obey the laws for our life and peace. If we do not stop at a red light, we know what will happen to us.

Now, do we keep the laws on using highways? What about the law of God? We know that we will have life and prosperity if we observe the law of God. If we disobey the Law, we will experience death and adversity. Even though we know the Law is righteous and good, we cannot subject ourselves to the law of God. Contrary to our knowledge and wishes, we sin against God.

What is wrong with us? Our problem is that we are the slaves of sin by birth. As long as we are alive to the flesh, sin reigns over our bodies as it pleases. Sin, the foreign enemy, is our master. Both the Jews who have received the law of God and the Gentiles who do not have the Law are under sin. We are forced to do his will and compelled to do evil things. The cruel taskmaster imposes hard labor on us. Our lives and bodies are in forced labors for sin. To carry out the evil desires of our flesh, we present the members of our bodies to obey the various lusts and pleasures of the flesh. Thus, we serve sin, though we do not want to. This is our dilemma: We the captives have no freedom to love and serve God and neighbors. We wish to serve the Law but do evil. Our hearts desire to be free and to soar to heaven and fly, but we are under the captivity of sin.

When we are in the flesh, we cannot serve the Lord God. Our spirits wish to serve Him, but our flesh is hostile toward Him. We practice the evil that we do not wish to do. In fact, we the slaves of sin are not able to subject to the law of God.

We know we ought to love our neighbors, but we have no freedom to love them. We cannot forgive those who sin against us. We are in captivity of self and have no freedom to look out for the interests of others. When we use our freedom for fleshly desires, we serve sin as slaves. We use the freedom of speech to hurt others by gossips and slander. Sexual liberation is slavery to sexual immorality. Human rights for fleshly lusts and pleasures are deceitful privileges to sin. We commit shameless deeds in slavery to sin.

Spending Life in Sins

Enslaved to sin, we spend our lives in various sins. Our eyes are full of envy, covetousness, jealousy, and pornography. Our tongues and lips speak boasting, arrogance, malicious and slanderous gossips, unkind words, deception, and falsehood. Our hands are given to stealing. Our bodies are presented to adultery and immorality. Our hearts are filled with hatred, pride, and murder.

The spirit of slavery is to fear all things. Through fear of death, we live out our whole lives in slavery to sin. We are oppressed under the yoke of slavery. Our souls are humbled with the labors for sin, and we are ashamed and embarrassed with evil works.

From the labors for sin, we find no rest for our souls. Our bodies are weary and our lives are bitter. Our souls are pierced and bruised by sin. Our spirits are wasted away and our vitality is drained away through our groaning. We sigh in this house of bondage to sin. We are despondent from cruel slavery to sin. Our souls stumble under the heavy burdens of sin and guilt. We are broken down and downtrodden.

The Dead in Sin

Sin is deadly. We sinners die for our sin, because sin has the sting of death like poison snakes.

Death is neither the end of all nor annihilation, just as life is not mere existence. It is the loss of life; consequently, it is the lack of life. When we sin and die, we become lifeless. We suffer the lack of all things of life: there is no peace, no joy, or no glory in our souls. Our souls without peace are restless. Our lives without joy are miserable. Our images without glory are wretched. Death brings tears from our eyes, and mourning and pain in our souls. Our lives are too painful to live with the pain of death. Condemned to death, we the prisoners in the dungeon sit in the darkness of death. But there is none to help us. Having no hope without God in the world, we cry out to the Lord our God for help in our distress.

In an account of his experience as a man in the flesh of sin, the apostle Paul cried out in the agony of death, "What a wretched man I am! Who will rescue me from this body of death?" The dead man turned to Jesus Christ our Savior for help in his trouble. John Bunyan, in one of his books, told how he was in such agony for nearly eighteen months. One day he went out to the fields with a heavy, troubled heart to see geese freely grazing on the fields. He was envious of the animals without the burdens of death.

Graduating from university, I was free from the eyes of my parents and the discipline of school. I used my freedom for fleshly lusts and pleasures. Freely I went out many nights and roamed in the darkness of Seoul to seek the pleasures in the world. Born of the flesh in the bondage of sin, the slave of sin served the master for various lusts and pleasures. The sinister power ruled me and I spent my life in all kinds of sin. Sin pierced and scarred my soul with many pangs. I was wounded and bleeding. From the cruel slavery of sin, my body was abused and left nothing sound. My soul knew pain and sorrow. Sin afflicted me with unrelieved and relentless labors, and I stumbled under the heavy burden of death. Finally, my soul fainted and fell into darkness.

Sin plundered all the precious things of my life. I went out full but became empty. I gave my body to serve sin and sin made my life a waste. As forest fires leave a wasteland of scorched earth and blackened trees, sin left my life in destruction and ruins. The lusts in my flesh burned me down to ashes. When I saw my life in ruins, I found no rest for my soul. In the anguish of death, I groaned within myself. Looking at my image of wretchedness and my life of misery, I could no longer bear the sufferings of my life. So miserable was my life that I longed for no further life. In a moment of despondency, I despaired of my life. I was a distraught man and despised my life even to death.

It took me one year to realize that my way of life in Seoul was not really the way to life. Through the sufferings of death, I came to my senses by increased awareness to the hidden tremors of my soul. I inquired about the problems of my life in the renaissance after my dark ages. Faced with the problem of death, I found nothing of help in the world. I was in trouble.

4. Poverty

Nakedness
> *The Clothed Yet Naked*
> *Sin Uncovers Our Nakedness*
> *The Shame of Nakedness*
> *Coverings*
> *The Dead in Nakedness*

Defilement
> *The Clean and the Unclean*
> *The Stained by the World*
> *The Defiled by Sin*
> *The Dead in Defilement*
> *The Unclean and Afflicted in Distress*

Hunger and Thirst
> *A Famine on the Heartland*
> *A Famine for the Word of God*
> *The Hungry and Thirsty Soul*
> *Not Finding the Word of God in the World*
> *The Poor Die with Hunger and Thirst*

Homelessness

We say in our hearts, "I'm rich and do not need a thing." But we do not realize that we are poor and needy. Life is more than clothes, food, and houses: it is the righteousness, love, peace, and joy of God. Without those things of God, our souls are poor and afflicted in the lack of all things.

When we do not serve the Lord our God with joy for the abundance of His life but love the world and serve sin, we serve our enemies in poverty—that is, in nakedness, in defilement, in hunger and thirst, and in homelessness.

Nakedness

The Clothed Yet Naked

You know well that your body needs clothing. You spend money for clothes and your closet is full of fine clothes. You put them on your body so that the nakedness of your body may not be exposed. Sometimes you adorn yourself with fashionable, trendy finery. You have confidence to stand before people. Fine clothing, however, does not make the person of your heart beautiful, because you are more than clothes.

Did you know that *you* need clothing? Now look at the person of your heart and see if you are naked. If you do not wear clothes for your soul, you are naked though you are clothed in outward appearances. God bestowed the splendor of His life for our souls to wear. As a mother covers the nakedness of her child with clothes, our Father God clothes us with a robe of His righteousness and adorns us with His glory. If you are not wearing the holy attire, the robe of purity and holiness, you are naked. You walk about naked.

Sin Uncovers Our Nakedness.

God bestowed us with the garments of His life and glory to cover our nakedness. When we sin against God, however, our eyes are opened and we realize that we are naked. Our nakedness is uncovered by our sin; we are naked before God.

Sin leaves us bare. As wanton women expose their nakedness in adultery, we love the world instead of our Husband God and uncover our nakedness through our adultery with our lovers. Our lovers strip us of our clothing, take away the beauty of life, leave us bare, and expose our nakedness. Our eyes see our nakedness, and we are aware of our sin and shame.

The Shame of Nakedness

When God joined Adam and Eve in marriage, the man and his wife were both naked and yet were not ashamed. In fact, they looked very good in the sight of God, because God bestowed them with the robe of His life and glory to cover their nakedness. We were also bare when we came into the world from our mothers' wombs. Yet we looked beautiful in the eyes of our mothers. When man and wife are one body clothed with love, they are naked and yet not ashamed.

Nevertheless, there are days when we put on clothing but are still naked and feel the shame of nakedness. When we sin, sin takes away the glory of life from us. Our nakedness is uncovered; the shame of our nakedness is exposed. There is no glory or splendor in our lives. We sin in secret, but our shame of nakedness is exposed before God and people. We are an open shame. God and people see our nakedness and scandalousness. Our glory has changed into shame. We are ashamed and embarrassed to lift up our faces to God and our neighbors. Because of our shame, we cannot enter into the holy place of God. We cannot stand in the assembly of saints.

Coverings

When Adam and Eve disobeyed the word of God and sinned against God, their eyes were opened and they realized that they were naked. They were ashamed and embarrassed to stand naked before God. Being afraid of the Lord God, they did two things: First, they made loin coverings for themselves by sewing fig leaves together to cover up their nakedness. Second, they hid themselves from the presence of God among the trees of the Garden of Eden.

When we realize we are naked by our sin, we do not want our sin and the shame of our nakedness to be revealed. We are afraid of God and people. Like Adam and Eve, we make ourselves coverings for our sin and nakedness, and hide ourselves. We wear masks and construct facades. We wear facemasks to cover our faces and put on hypocrisy for our souls. We pretend to be somebody else. Many religious people hold to a form of godliness and show false humility. As those who had surgeries wear long dresses or pants to cover the scars, we cover up the wounds of our sin. We live like snails, not wanting anyone see our nakedness.

We hide our evil deeds in our hearts. Then, we keep silent about our sins and nakedness in the fear of open shame before others. We have secrets in our hearts, run as fugitives to find a hiding place, and stand some distance away from our neighbors and hide from God's presence. Sinners are restless fugitives.

In the days of my nakedness and shame, I feared people might find me out and lived with the terror of open shame. So I hid my sins deep down in my heart and kept silent about my sinfulness. I did not go out of the doors of my heart. I wore facemasks of my own making to cover up the secrets of my heart. They were ill-fitting and awkward, and made my life very uncomfortable. My life was unreal.

When I concealed my sins, the burdens of my secrets and pretension were heavy on me. My vitality was drained away and I could not see the prosperity of life. I found no peace or rest in my soul. I was burdened since I did not want to be naked. I groaned, longing to be clothed with the glory of life. Like a bride without a wedding gown, I went about in the pain of nakedness.

The Dead in Nakedness

Those without the garment of God's righteousness die, just as the naked die for the lack of a covering in the frigid streets. The naked put on clothing for their bodies but their hearts do not have the warmth of love. They are dead and cold.

We see that even the rich with earthly possessions die in exposure like the poor, because they cannot redeem their lives from nakedness and death. Experiencing the pain of death, they long to be clothed with the glory of life. They are restless until they put on the righteousness of God.

Do you know where to buy the garment of God's righteousness?

The naked will go here and there to seek the robe of holiness, but will not find it in the world. On that evil day, the poor and naked will die without life. The needy will cry out to God in their trouble, "Cover me, or I perish."

Defilement

The Clean and the Unclean

We wash our bodies and clothes to be clean. And we make a distinction between the clean and the unclean and try to keep us clean. When we are clean and beautiful, we have confidence to stand before people in wholeness, perfection, and glory.

How blessed is the person who is clean inside and outside! The pure in heart shall see God. The person with a clean heart has life and glory and has confidence to enter the holy place of God. The holy person worships and serves the Lord God with great joy.

The unclean in heart are not so. They have no confidence to enter the holy place because of an evil conscience and stand far away from holy God. They are ashamed and embarrassed before God for their sin and uncleanness and are unwilling to lift up their eyes to God. God has no regard for the unclean and their offerings and sacrifices to Him. The defiled multiply prayers with dirty hands, but God does not listen.

How can a person be defiled and unclean? Just as pure honey becomes impure when the different material of sugar is mixed, the impure admixture of sin defiles the person. As dirt defiles the body and clothing, the world and sin make the person unclean.

The Stained by the World

To be clean, we are to love the Lord God only. When we love the world rather than our God, we become unclean, as adulterers/adulteresses are unclean. We defile our souls with our idols. As the bride of the Lord God, we are to love Him and no one else to be pure. If we love the world, however, we are unfaithful brides. When our minds are set on the things of the world and we go after our lovers, we defile ourselves with adultery with them. We are stained by the world. Many religious people try to hold the world in one hand and God in the other. But they are double-minded and impure.

The Defiled by Sin

Sin defiles the sinner.

When we present the members of our bodies to serve sin, the impurity of sin defiles us. Evil things—for example, pride, envy, coveting, hatred, and anger—in our hearts make us impure. Our eyes for lustful look on a man, a woman, or pornography (e.g., dirty magazines and videos) make us dirty. Our mouths for gossips, foul language, and dirty jokes make us unclean. Our untamed tongues defile our entire bodies. When we touch dirty money, we become unclean.

Adultery pollutes the adulterers. People know the dangers of HIV, AIDS, and venereal diseases. Yet they change sexual partners like work-clothes. They count adultery as a pleasure, but it is defilement. Those who claim human rights in choosing sexual orientation and commit indecent acts are in the shame of impurity.

At the times of unbelief and ignorance, we are senseless. Like a pig wallowing in the mire of clay, we are soiled with the mire of sin. Nothing is pure: our bodies, minds, and consciences are sordid. We have ruined ourselves with the uncleanness of sin.

Having seen the glory of God and his uncleanness, Isaiah, a prophet of God, cried, "Woe to me! I am ruined! For I am a man of unclean lips." Peter, a disciple of Jesus, was defiled by sin, so that no one could touch him. He said to the Lord Jesus, "Go away from me, Lord; I am a sinful man!"

When we are unclean, our lives are useless like soiled clothes. We are good for nothing, neither for God nor for ourselves. In the lack of purity and glory, we are poor. We are in shame and dishonor.

The Dead in Defilement

A contaminated lake has no life; pollution kills life in the lake. When the body in which we live is polluted with sin, we have no life. The lakes of our hearts are dead from the pollution of sin.

Love as well as water must flow to have life. Love for God and neighbors must flow from the heart for life. As a lake where water does not flow out of becomes a dead lake (e.g., the Dead Sea), a heart where love, peace, and joy do not flow from is dead. The dam of selfishness makes the heart corrupt and dead. The dead feel restless even when they do nothing.

We infect the sanctuaries of our bodies with the terrible disease of sin. We defile the holy temples of God with sin, and our bodies are filthy. Our glories are ruined and our lives lie useless. Our souls mourn the lives in ruins.

When days are filled with filthiness and misery, the unclean long to be washed and renewed. They live like lepers, who are separated from the living and live in the shadow of death. Naaman, the captain of ancient Syrian army, was a great, honorable man, but he was a leper. The loathsome disease, leprosy, made him unclean. He longed to be washed and groaned for cleanness.

The Unclean and Afflicted in Distress

How can filthy sinners be washed to be clean? We can wash ourselves from dirt with water and detergents, but cannot remove the stain of sin with the things of the world. No bleachers in the world can whiten it, nor can our good works in the world. In fact, none in the world can cleanse the defilement of sin.

There are many types of purification in the world's religions. Various modes of baptism—for example, sprinkling, pouring, and immersing—are practiced in Christian churches. The effects of water baptism are debated among churches. Some claim to receive the Holy Spirit through water baptism. Many churches require it to become church members and officials. Some assert other strange things.

In all the types, modes, and effects of baptism, one thing is common: man baptizes with water. Water baptism cannot make worshipers perfect in conscience; water can remove dirt from the body but cannot wash the defilement of sin or evil conscience. Water baptism cannot wash sinners to have a pure heart, a good conscience, and a sincere faith before God. The rite of baptism in the Christian church is not the reality of washing but the testimony of having been washed by the Holy Spirit through Jesus Christ. Those who are baptized with natural water have no confidence to enter the holy place of God; their hearts are still unclean.

Unclean souls seek washing and renewal, but they will not find it in the world. When life is filled with defilement, death, and misery, they long to be washed by God. The poor, helpless sinners cry out to the Lord God in their distress, "Wash me, or I die. Renew me, O God. I will live a new life."

When I followed the lusts of the flesh in the night streets of Seoul, the stormy wind of pleasures plunged me into the bog of sin. There I wallowed in the mire of sin, became filthy, and messed up my precious life. My purity was ruined in the defilement of sin. I made efforts to come out of the bog many times, but I was helplessly sinking further down into the depth of the bog. Bereft of purity and innocence, I was left with nothing clean. I was in dishonor and in ruins. There was no glory in my life. Instead, I saw my wretched image and loathed myself for all the evil things that I had done. As my soul sank under the heavy burdens of defilement, I saw myself sinking helplessly downward into the abyss of darkness. At the deep valley of death, the current of darkness engulfed me. On that day, I feared for my life and was in danger of perishing. So I set my heart on fleeing from the city of defilement and destruction.

One day in the spring of 1969, my heart overflowed with the mourning of death during my lunch hour. The tumult of my heart rushed me out of my office and I went out into the garden. Having none to save me out of my trouble, I lifted up my eyes to the heaven for help. Out of a clear sky, Dr. Hong Seong-ok appeared before me and told me about an opportunity for teaching at the Department of Forestry, Seoul National University, in Suwon. To my amazement and my delight, the position was offered to me. Immediately I escaped for safety from Seoul to Suwon. It was a miraculous, great escape.

No sooner had I arrived in Suwon than I walked along a familiar path in a forest near the campus with my eyes downcast and a heavy, troubled heart. When my heart groaned with ruined life and was surged with an evil conscience, I slowly came to a stop at one point.

Suddenly in a vision, I saw myself as a ruined man in defilement. My cleverness failed to give me the glory of life that I had hoped for. It only led me to a life ruined with impurities. My searches for the joy of life in the world left me with sorrow and pain only. Then I grieved over the loss of my purity and innocence. I asked myself, "How on earth could such an innocent man like me becomes this filthy man? What shall I do with a wretched man like me?" And I cried, "Oh, what a foolish man I am! I'm ruined!" With the bitterness of death in my soul, I lamented over my ruins. My soul melted away in my misery. Then, the billows of sorrow rolled over me and I was unable to control the raging tide of sorrow. It poured out my broken heart like water and a rush of tears flooded my eyes and my face.

When I was awakened from the vision, I found myself standing in the university nursery (tree seedlings), the place where I saw the blue sky of my young dreams as a student. As my soul sank down into the darkness of death and my body cleaved to earth, I kneeled to the ground and scooped up a handful of dirt in my hands. Squeezing the dirt with my hands and lifting up my eyes toward the heaven, I poured out my soul within me and cried out in anguish, "Wash me, and I will be a new person." And I wept bitterly.

Hunger and Thirst

You look for the satisfaction of life, as we all do. You work hard to gain the world and spend money for the things on earth. You eat, but are still hungry. You drink, but are not satisfied.

Do you know why? Consider your ways to life. Your ways are good education, skills, and hard work with good heart. You have sown much for an abundant harvest and sought the satisfaction of life in the good things of earth.

Stop toiling at your work now and look at your heart. What do you see?

A Famine on the Heartland

A farmer hopes for a bumper crop. He looks for good soil, improved seed, advanced skills, and newer equipment. Then he does all the labors of tilling, sowing, and culturing with his hands. Beyond all these things, however, he first seeks the season of rain. His eyes are always on the sky for the seasonal rain. While he works with hardships and patience, the soil drinks the rain from the sky and produces life and fruit useful to the farmer. At harvest time, he sees the fruit of his labors and rejoices in abundance.

The farmer does not hope for a plentiful harvest without seasonal rains on the land. No matter how hard and skillfully he works, if the sky withholds its rain, the land will withhold its produce. There will be a famine on the land. When a famine comes over the land, the farmer will suffer for the lack of all things. There is no water or food. The poor farmer will die with hunger and thirst. The prodigal son in Jesus' parable went to a distant country to seek the life in the world, far from his father. When he spent everything and a severe famine occurred in the country, he was poor and needy. He was dying with hunger.

Do you know your heartland needs the rain out of heaven to produce life? As the land needs the rain of the sky to produce life, you need the rain of heaven to have life. The land of valleys by the stream of water can be irrigated by human labor, but the land of hills should drink the rain of the sky. Your body can be nourished with your efforts, like the land of valleys. By your toils of occupation, you buy the produce of earth. You take care of your body by eating food and drinking water. On the other hand, your heartland must drink the rain out of heaven. God's eyes are always on your heartland. To those who obey the Lord Jesus, God gives the rain of heaven for life and prosperity.

When did you open your heart to the Lord Jesus and receive the living water from heaven? If you have rejected the word of God and did not drink the rain of heaven, your heartland will not produce life. When you have had a drought on your heartland for years, you have a famine on your heartland.

A Famine for the Word of God

A famine on the heartland is not a famine of water and food but a famine of hearing the word of God. Hearing the word of God is not merely hearing it by the ears but receiving it into the heart by faith.

At the time of the Old Testament of the Bible, God warned through His prophet Amos of the days of judgment when He will send a famine for the word of God. Now in these last days of the world, God has spoken His word to us by His Son Jesus. Jesus declared, "I am the bread of life. He who comes to me will never go hungry, and he who believes in me will never be thirsty." God sends the rain of heaven abundantly through Jesus Christ; accordingly, we must come to Jesus Christ to receive the living water. When we reject Jesus Christ, the word of God, we do not receive the rain out of heaven. The drought and famine for the word of God come on our heartlands. Our lives dry up like a parched land and do not yield the fruit of life. Our lives are a barren waste. In the lack of all things for life, our souls long for the living water, like a parched land thirst for water. Deep down inside our souls, we feel a hunger for love and peace, and a thirst for joy. I know you feel the hunger and thirst; so did I.

As I entered the thirty-fourth year of my life, I was aware of a famine on my heartland. The famine was so severe that it sparked an evaluation of my ways and works in the world. For the abundant harvest of life, I have sown much knowledge and labor. So far, I have cultured my life by establishing a career, finding a job, and starting a family. I expected my life to produce good fruit in abundance by now. When I looked for the fruit of life in my life, to my disappointment, I found nothing on it except leaves only. My life did not yield the good fruit of love, peace, and joy for me. Instead, it yielded only worthless ones: the thorns of anxiety, the thistles of worry in the world, and the briars of doubts and fear. My soul was empty like chaff (grain covering without the fruit of life inside). My life looked substantial on the outside but contained nothing inside. It had the outward appearance of life with the things of the world, but did not have the good fruit of life. I was bitterly disappointed with my life without fruit, like an orchard owner looking at autumn fruit trees without fruits. I toiled in vain. I realized I was advancing in age without obtaining life. One season after another, I was getting older but was not growing up to maturity and bearing the fruit of life. My life was useless and worthless. I was insecure in all my ways like fallen leaves driven by the wind.

When a famine for the word of God comes over our heartlands, we are not satisfied with what we have, however wealthy we are. The Samaritan woman in the Bible, the Gospel according to John, sought the satisfaction of life in men. She was obsessed with finding love in order to have life. She loved men for life and pursued her lovers in the belief that men will give her the satisfaction of life. Even having drunken love from six men, she was still thirsty. She drank the water from the well, but was still thirsty for life.

My tongue loved the taste of good food from earth, but my heart abhorred the word of God. My sole care was to fill my belly with the good things on earth. Often I dined out at restaurants in Vancouver to eat such delicacies as bird's nest soup, *sashimi*, and *filet mignon*. I drank old, rotten liquors, as the saying goes, the older the better. Yet none of them satisfied me whenever I saw emptiness in my heart.

It is our folly to look for the satisfaction of life in the abundance of earthly things. We eat all sorts of things with greed, for example, food, books, money, houses, cars, lands, properties, and pleasures. Our hearts, being unsatisfied, desire ever more and larger. All the time we eat, but no one is full enough to say, "No more." We have many goods laid up for years to come, but there is never enough to be satisfied. One who eats of earthly things and is filled with them temporally and partially will hunger again; earthly things do not endure to eternal life but perish.

Human heart cannot be filled with food, nor be warmed with clothes, nor be secure with houses. Human life is not eating, clothing, or housing but peace, love, and joy. We are truly happy when our hearts are filled with the heavenly, eternal things of God.

If we want more from the world to be satisfied with our lives, we will never say, "Enough." Our eyes are not satisfied with what we see. Not being content, we want more and more. We wish, "If I had this and that." We say, "If only I had more money, I'd be happy." Oh, yes, money can buy happiness. We increase wealth and get happier as we get richer. Money, however, has the power to delight human heart only temporally and partially. We can increase our bank accounts with money, but we will still hunger again. Money can buy many things of earth, but it cannot buy the true things of life. We can buy a monster house but not a peaceful home, warm clothing but not a warm heart of love, pleasures and laughs but not a joyful heart, and plentiful food but not a satisfied soul. Money cannot fill human heart, nor can it satisfy human soul. Although we gain the whole world, we will not be satisfied with our lives. Man needs more than the riches of the world to have the satisfaction of life. Human heart is empty until God fills it with Himself. God has set eternity in man's heart; God alone can satisfy man's heart with His eternity. Only eternal God can fill the void in human heart.

The Hungry and Thirsty Soul

The famine in my heartland wreaked havoc on my soul with hunger and thirst. And I saw the ravages of famine in my soul. When I reached my thirty-fifth year, the midpoint in my journey to heaven if the years of life are seventy, my soul was impoverished by famine. I had set out my journey full of dreams and plans, but my life was empty and gnawing me with an aching void. I began to be in a dire need. I felt the pang of hunger and thirst, and began to be in a desperate need. It was so unbearable to live with the intense pangs of starvation that death seemed better to me. I could not continue to live on another thirty-five years. It seemed to me that my remaining years on the earth will fleet away like the passing clouds. Though my age will be advanced, my life will remain the same as it has been until I die. Then I said to myself, "If life is like this, it is worthless to live on the rest of my years upon the earth." I did not want to continue living a life of wretchedness and misery for another thirty-five years. Oh, I wished that I would rather have seven days of a life filled with peace and joy than live a long life of hunger and thirst. Through the pains of hunger and thirst in my soul, I learned that man does not live by earthly things alone. Earthly food did not give the life of peace and joy to me. The sufferings of poverty awakened me from sleep in darkness to be aware of my need for the word of God, the food of eternal life. At last, I began to seek God's word.

Not Finding the Word of God in the World

In the days of famine, the poor and needy turn everywhere for help. They go here and there to seek the word of God. Some go to India, some to Yukon, some to the remote area far from their situations. But they do not find it.

Some turn to philosophy for the wisdom of life but do not find it there. Philosophers pursue it in their minds by their intellect and cleverness. Hence, philosophy is human wisdom at its best. Human wisdom does not understand the wisdom of God in a mystery.

Hungry souls try the world's religions: Judaism, Christianity, Islam, Buddhism, Hinduism, and so forth. But they do not find the word of God there. The poor and afflicted seek the food of heaven for their souls, but there is none. The world's religions are not according to Jesus Christ but according to men. Man-made religions have a form of godliness, but they give nothing for a hungry soul.

Thirsty souls come to the church of God for the word of God. They have their ears tickled with the messages of men. Their bodies are busy with the programs of worship, prayer, Bible study, social gathering, evangelism and foreign mission, and also with attending committees and meetings. They do good works for the poor in the world. Nevertheless, their souls will be still thirsty unless they drink the word of God. They keep hearing the showers of the living water from heaven, but their hearts remain dry. They go home with thirsty souls after church.

You search the Bible to find the word of God. The Bible bears witness of Jesus as the Son of God and the Christ. If you are unwilling to come to Him, you will not find the word of God. You have come short of God's word, Jesus Christ.

The Poor Die with Hunger and Thirst

When we do not find the word of God, the evil day comes to us. Our souls faint from hunger and thirst, fall into the pit of death, and do not rise again; there is none in the world to raise us up.

The tragic death of the poor would seem to belong to the poor beggars living on the streets. Yet it happens to the rich in the world. The rich die without God's word. Their riches will not deliver their souls from death. When I passed through the streets of Vancouver's Downtown Eastside and noticed a destitute beggar, I stopped to watch him. He had no food or shelter. The poor man reeled here and there in the city to seek the food of life. On the day when he could not find it, he died alone in a deserted place. The poor beggar reminded me of my condition. I appeared to him to be rich on the outside, but I was dying with hunger inside. I silently murmured, "Who will know the pains of hunger in my soul and help me?" By the time my thoughts came this far, I was lost in darkness.

We eat to live, but we all die. The young, the rich, the clever, and the mighty—all die not for the lack of food and drink but for the lack of the word of God. We reject the word of God and have famine in our heartlands. We die with hunger and thirst.

Although my soul died with hunger and thirst, I continued stubbornly to reject the word of God and did not receive the living water out of heaven. Finally, my heartland became like barrens. As my life wasted away, I became acutely aware of the suffering and pain of poverty in my soul. Death was well known to my soul. The problem of death posed great difficulties to my pilgrimage to heaven.

When my soul died, all things were meaningless to me. I lost the meaning of life. Everything that I had once valued was discounted as nothing. Earthly possessions meant nothing to me. What good was a house full of furniture if my home was empty? When I did not have life, what good were cars to me? I kicked the foundation of my house and the tires of my cars out of frustration with my life. The good things of the world became insignificant. They profited my soul nothing and no longer meant anything. I had no delight in the things that I formerly treasured for my life. When I saw no joy in my heart, there was no purpose for my life. On weekend mornings, I had no reason to get up. Seeing the emptiness of my soul, I was disillusioned with my life.

Faced with the crisis of death in my life, I had to do something. I resolved to undertake a quest for a solution to my problem of death. In the hope that there must be a place where my hungry and thirsty soul could be satisfied, I set out to find the place. My soul knew poverty and pain but did not know where to turn for help. First I turned to the world but could not find help there. Being desperate in my plight, I resigned from my position in the consulting company for the pulp and paper industry and began to seek a solution to the problem of death. Having no hope in the world, I hoped in God. Now God was my only hope.

As a last resort, I turned to the Bible to seek the word of God. (Grace and I exchanged the Bibles as gifts for our engagement at my suggestion. But I did not open my Bible and it was just collecting dust. I knew nothing about the Bible except a vague idea that it is a good book.)

One Monday morning in 1976, I came up to Capilano Canyon in Vancouver to find the solitude of the forest. Away from everything in the world, I walked along a wooded trail by the river with the Bible in my hand. I found a boulder by the water and sat and read the Bible. With the desperation of a man dying with hunger, I searched the Bible to find the word of life.

God in the Old Testament seemed to me to be the God of Israel, not of Koreans. So I opened the New Testament and turned to the Gospel according to Matthew. The gospel of Jesus Christ began with the genealogy of Jesus Christ the son of David, the son of Abraham. "Abraham was the father of Isaac, Isaac the father of Jacob, Jacob the father of ..." On and on, it continued to list foreign, unfamiliar names.

Among the many names, I could not find Kim, my family name. The passage was dry, boring, and irrelevant. So I skipped it.

The virgin birth of a son Jesus recorded in the following passage appeared to me as nonsense, and I would not believe it. I fortified my lofty stronghold of worldly wisdom and stood up against the word of God with hostility. Soon my heart became a battleground. While I was struggling to suppress the word of God with unbelief, the sword of God's word pierced far into the depth of my inner being with many pangs. My soul was lacerated, wounded, and bleeding. When I disobeyed the word of God with unbelief, it spelled judgment for me. The word of God brought destruction to my soul.

As the days went by, I had to face more of Jesus' miracles—namely, healing the sick, calming the stormy sea, exorcising, feeding five thousand, and walking on the water. By Thursday I became very weary from the battle against the word of God. My reading speed gradually diminished. My eyesight grew dimmer and I could not see well.

Homelessness

As you know, we need a home for life. The home is the dwelling place of family, a place of love and fellowship, a place to sleep and rest, a place to eat and get laundry done, and a shelter at the time of storm.

You dream to dwell in a good house and seek a larger house. You have worked hard and have built a house for yourself. You have filled it with the good things on earth—namely, rooms with furniture; pantry, fridge, and freezer with food; closets and chests with clothes; and garage with cars. You are dwelling in your house with ease.

Look, you have a house for your body but do not have a house for your soul. Your body is the dwelling place of your soul. The house of your body is also a temple of God. The temple of God is God's dwelling place. He fills it with His glory, and there are love, fellowship, peace, and rest in it. God meets His people there. There the people of God approach God with worship. There you have fellowship with God and His people. God hears your prayers offered in the house of God.

Therefore, the temple of God is essential for your life and glory, just as your body needs an earthly house for life.

The unbelieving and ignorant carelessly profane the house of God by abusing it for others. We make it a den of sin; some, a smoking factory; some, a drinking tavern; some, a house of merchandise; and the like. If we abuse the sanctuary of God, God will destroy our houses in which we live. The houses for our souls lie in ruins, and we become homeless. We have no place to meet God, worship Him, and pray to Him. We have no home to go when the world becomes dark and the night comes. As the homeless, we wander in the world. On an evil day, we will face death and adversity.

Now look at the house of your body in which your soul dwells. If it lies desolate without the life and glory of God, you are poor and homeless.

5. Wilderness

The Wandering in the Wilderness

Introduction

This world is not a place for us to settle permanently; we are aliens and sojourners. We are pilgrims seeking the eternal, heavenly country and go through this world on our ways to the promised life of God in heaven. We camp at an address for a little while and then continue on our journeys to the destination of heaven.

The world through which we travel is the wilderness. It is a dry, weary land where there is no living water. There is no path to life in it; it is a place of wandering and getting lost. There are dangers of deadly poisonous snakes and scorpions. It is a place where demonic powers howl. It is a land of deserts and death. Besides, there are pits of destruction and perishing.

At the times of unbelief, we do not know the right way that we must go or how to go out or come in the wilderness of the world. Like sheep, we need a shepherd for guidance, provision, and protection. Jesus Christ is the Shepherd of our souls. He shows us the way through the world and leads us to the place of water and rest. He guides us in the path of righteousness and life, provides for our needs, and protects us from all the dangers of the world.

The Separated from the Lord Our Shepherd

The unbelievers do not know the Shepherd Jesus or the way in Him. Their hearts wander from Jesus Christ, and they set out their journeys through the wilderness of the world along their own ways. Being separated from the Shepherd, they go astray to the wrong ways of unrighteousness and ungodliness.

A person without Jesus Christ is like a sheep without a shepherd. The person does not find the righteous way to life and wanders in the wilderness of sin.

The Wandering in the Wilderness of Sin

When I did not know the Shepherd Jesus, I followed the stubbornness of my unbelieving heart and entered the wilderness of sin. Having been separated far from the Shepherd, I could not find the path to life and prosperity and wandered in the wilderness of sin.

My pilgrimage to heaven through the world was attended with the adversity and hardship of the wilderness. Being lost in the wilderness of sin, I wandered aimlessly many years. My soul was hungry and thirsty. The intense heat of the burning sun was striking on my head. The scorching heat of the wilderness was beating on my body and wasted away my strength; I was weary. The prickling briers of sin wounded my soul and pierced my body. My soul and body had many scars. I stumbled over the rocks of sin and my soul was bruised, torn, and swollen. There was nothing sound in me. Through the hardship of the wilderness, I learned the difficulties of life.

Many times I made efforts to change my way of life and went from city to city. I moved to many places in a quest for a new and better life and saw some changes of scenery. But I continued wandering in sin and darkness. I floundered around for a way through the desolate land of the world. Wandering through the mountains and valleys within the confines of my world, I circled many times, always coming back to the point of zero again and again. The course of my life repeated itself without reaching anywhere. I did not make any progress toward the destination of heaven. I was lost in the middle of nowhere and stood disoriented. Thus, I remained in the dreadful wilderness of sin for many years.

As the years went by, my soul became like a wilderness; my life was barren and desolate. It was weary for me to see the wandering man. Despite journeying from childhood and youth to adulthood, I could not enter life and prosperity. Those years were a time of waste life, as I spent my life in sin. When I wandered further and further away from the life of God in Jesus Christ, I entered a desert region in the wilderness.

The Lost in the Desert

Overview

The wanderers in the wilderness of sin will be lost in a desert, the region of death. They will lose their souls (lives) through death, in exile far from the life of God. To love the world is to lose one's soul; to live without Jesus Christ is to lose one's life. Jesus Christ said, "What good will it be for a man if he gains the whole world, yet forfeits his soul? Or what can a man give in exchange for his soul?" Jesus' parable of "the prodigal son" portrays the one who seeks the pleasures of the world, is separated from God the Father, and is lost in the world. The prodigal son was dying with hunger in far country, repented, and returned to his father's house. The father said, "This son of mine was dead and is alive again; he was lost and is found." The son went far away from the father of life to the world and was lost in the desert of the world.

The Living Dead

The living dead are the dead while they are still alive. Their bodies are alive, but their souls are dead. They are still talking and walking, but they experience spiritual death with a conscience of its pain. Their existence in spiritual death is a great trouble for their souls. The separation of sin has caused their death. To be separated by sin from God is to be lost from the life of God. Just as the body without the spirit is dead, the soul without the Spirit of God is dead. Those without the Holy Spirit of life are spiritually dead.

God commanded Adam, "You must not eat from the tree of the knowledge of good and evil, for when you eat of it you will surely die." When Adam and Eve disobeyed the word of God and ate the fruit of the tree, immediately their souls died because of their sins. They were still alive physically. Lost from the Garden of Eden, the blessed life of God, their souls experienced the sufferings of death. They lived a life of the living dead in the world for years, and eventually their bodies died and returned to the ground. When the apostle Paul sinned against God and experienced spiritual death, the living dead man cried out, "What a wretched man I am! Who will rescue me from this body of death?" The cry of a sinner experiencing death testifies to the reality of a life of death. The Bible says, "The widow who lives for pleasure is dead even while she lives." Those who give themselves to wanton pleasure are dead. The Lord Jesus said to the church in Sardis, "You have a reputation of being alive, but you are dead." The church without the Spirit of God is dead even though the people are congregating, talking, praying, and singing. A church without the warmth of love in the Spirit of God is dead and cold.

We do not have to die physically to taste death. Nor do we need to wait for our bodily deaths to enter hell. When we sin, we taste death and hell while we are still alive here and now. We experience a living hell.

When I wandered in the world of sin far away from the Lord God of life, I could not enter eternal life and was lost in the desert. I did not know the way of peace and rest; my soul was restless and weary. My life was a living hell. The sufferings of my spiritual death were far worse beyond all comparison to my physical death. This is because my soul was separated by my sin from God and entered a living hell through my spiritual death. On the other hand, my spirit was separated from my body through my physical death. When I was still a youth, I suffered an acute typhoid fever for three days. Then my spirit rose out of my body and entered misty clouds. I felt the profound sense of freedom and peace, which was inexpressible with words. My physical death, however, brought travail and wailing to my parents. One day after my doctor abandoned all hope for my life and left me as a dead man, life came back to my body. Every cell in my body felt the sensation of refreshing by the spirit of life. It took three months for me to walk again.

The living dead are like deciduous trees in winter. One rainy morning in the early winter of 1990, I was driving through the Appalachian Mountains on my way to Toronto from Boston. The forest along the freeway appeared to me like a memorial park of trees. The trees were dead gray. The branches were naked without the life and splendor of their green leaves. There were no signs of life and prosperity. There was no talking among the trees in the whisperings of life under the wind. All was deathly silence. The scenery of the living dead trees—not dead but dormant—was chilly and hair-raising.

The living dead see neither life nor prosperity in their souls. They have no joyful songs in their hearts to sing to God, nor worship in their spirits. There are no life stories to tell others. They are quiet like a cemetery. When their hearts are filled with the sorrow and grief of death, they pour out tears through their eyes.

When we are dead spiritually and do not have the love of God, our hearts are as cold as a dead body. A corpse is cold and hard, wrapped in linen, put in a casket, and then buried in a dark grave. It is separated from the living, alone in the cemetery. Our hearts are still pumping warm blood, but they are cold and hard like a frozen lake. We put on clothing, but our hearts are not warm enough. We have no feelings of compassionate love and loving-kindness. We are cold-hearted and unloving. When our lives are unbearable with death, we cry out to the God of life, "Revive us."

The soul without the peace of God is solitary and lonely, just as a deceased person is separated from the living and is alone in the grave. The living dead person is alienated from the living God and does not have the fellowship of life with the living. Walking alone in the desolate life of the desert, the person comes to know that he or she is isolated from God and the living. No one crosses or dwells in the person's heart, the desert. It is a deserted, solitary, and lonely place.

Having nobody crossing in my heart of desert, I felt far away from the world of the living. I reflected on my alienation from the living and felt a sense of loneliness. In those times, I was alone in the grave of my body. It seemed to me that I was forsaken and left all alone in the universe. I no longer belonged to the world and was withdrawn and detached. Without the fellowship of peace, I did not know the peace of life. I sought rest from my works in the world, but could not find it; my heart was restless.

The living dead have a heart of stone. The dead, hardened heart is senseless and stubborn like a hard rock and will not respond to the call of God like a corpse. It will not obey the word of God. Even when we call the name of the beloved one, the deceased person will not respond. We shake the body to wake the person from the sleep of death, but the person cannot respond. The dead have lost freedom to do the things they ought to do. They know they ought to love their neighbors, but their hearts without sincere love are dead. Their hearts are all wrapped up in the linen of self-love and shut in the casket of ego, just as the corpse is wrapped in linen and imprisoned in the casket.

When my soul experienced death, I knew I was in trouble. I did not know the cause of death, but knew the wrongness of death. I could not accept death as an inevitable part of life. I said to myself, "There has got to be a better way to live. There must be a better life for man." I yearned to see the splendor of life.

A marriage without peace is dead, even while the husband and wife are still living together. They share one bed but do not see the beauty of union. They cannot touch each other because of their endless wars. There are the destruction, tears, and pain of death in their marriage.

I wished my home to be filled with peace, love, and joy. After work, I ran to my house to build up a happy home. While we dwelled in a house filled with earthly goods, our marriage without love was dead. I hoped for life and light in our home, but saw death and darkness. Contrary to my wishes for our marriage, I saw endless conflicts and disasters. Sunday mornings at our breakfast table, my wife talked about the God of the Bible. But I denied her God by talking about my belief in my supernatural Being. I rejected the God of churchgoers when I did not find the reality of their words in their lives. When I refused to believe in Jesus Christ and go to church with her, she became frustrated with me. In the final phase of our conflicts, we usually expressed our enmity toward each other by shooting the damaging missiles of evil words. Our battles were over when she ran to the master bedroom with overwhelming sorrow in her heart and tears on her face. She poured out her heart of weeping and lamenting over the bed. It was one thing for her to miss joyful worship services at church with the people of God on Sundays. It was another to live with her unbelieving husband. For my part, our disharmony frustrated my longing for a happy marriage. When I saw our broken marriage, I felt it became like a glass figurine that was shattered into pieces. For a short while, I did not know what to do about our broken relationship and just sat at the table with a troubled heart. When my heart became calm and soft, usually within half an hour, I went to comfort her with my apology and good words.

As a criminal condemned to death waits in a dark cell for the day of execution, the living dead wait for their physical deaths and then the second death in hell by the final judgment. In the meantime, their souls dwell in the darkness of death. When the misery and wretchedness of death in their souls become unbearable, they experience a living hell. Their souls are exposed to the heat of hell, parched with thirst, and tormented in the agony of the unbearable heat. The fire of hell consumes them and turns them to ashes. And they see the gray ashes of life. In those days when their lives are a living hell, they will seek death.

The Perishing in the Abyss of Hell

Definition of the Word "Perish"

To perish is for a person to become destroyed utterly or ruined completely by sin and death. The dead person in sin plunges into the abyss of darkness, perishes from the life and glory of God, and is no longer visible.

Do you know the perishing?

I know many of them. They are everywhere. The wise of the world yet without the knowledge of God perish like fools. They trust and boast their wisdom, yet perish without understanding. The rich also perish because they cannot redeem their souls from death with money. Those who walk on the way of success in the world without knowing the way leading to the country of God perish like failures. Good works will not be able to deliver the workers from perishing. One day Isaiah, a prophet of Israel, saw the glory of God and his perishing, and cried, "Woe to me! I am ruined!" God created man in His image and likeness, and crowned him with His life and glory. When the image of God is utterly ruined by sin and death, we are perishing. We lose the life and glory of God completely and perish in the abyss of hell.

I Was Once Perishing in the Abyss of a Living Hell

On the days when I was seeking the word of God in Capilano Canyon in Vancouver, I came to the Bible but could not find the word of God there. Yet I persevered in my determination to continue reading the Bible.

Friday morning I came up to the same place but had no courage to open the Bible. The wounds in my soul were too painful; I did not want the raw wounds to be lacerated by the word of God any more. While debating in my mind whether I should open and read the Bible or not, I repeated opening it and immediately closing it many times. The struggle continued until the late afternoon.

All of sudden, I fell into a trance and saw a vision. A poor, wretched traveler in a desert was slowly trudging in extreme weariness. His body was wasted away from the weariness of a long journey through the desert. He had wandered in the great and terrible desert without food and drink for a long time. He was hungry and thirsty. He was confused. He was staggering and reeling back and forth like a drunkard. The darkness of death was closing in and he could not see beyond one foot around him. He was trying to drag the dead weight of his body.

When I recognized the traveler as me, the darkness of death encompassed me completely. I could not go on my journey farther. My soul and body pined away under the heavy burdens of death, and I leaned and wiggled forward and sideways on the spot for a while. Then, my strength failed to drag the body of death. Eventually, my soul fainted within me, and I fell and plunged into the infinite, bottomless abyss filled with darkness. As I was descending into the abyss of death, black, deep darkness engulfed me, and I perished. At that moment, I knew I came to the end of my life. When I was younger, I survived many dangers of life by using my wits. This time, however, I was at my wit's end, with nothing remaining for me to do except to perish. When I realized that there was none to help me, my soul was terrified with the horror of perishing. I was in great distress.

Thus, my pilgrimage to heaven ended—in hell.

I do not know how long I was in the trance.

When I woke up from the trance and opened my eyes, I looked up to see my surroundings filled with white foggy clouds. As the clouds dissipated slowly and gradually to make a small opening of a tunnel before my eyes, I was barely able to see the blue sky through the tunnel. I was so weak that I could hardly sense anything; there was no strength left in my body like a man who has been sick with a terrible disease for a very long time. I do not know how I managed to walk along the trail in the canyon to the parking lot and drive home on that day.

Then I became extremely weak with a strange sickness. It took three days for me to sense my existence in the world. As a man after a fit of illness, I had to gather up my strength for several days after.

When I recovered from the sickness, I was awakened to the reality that I was the breadwinner for my family. I went back to work at the consulting company for the pulp and paper industry without finding the word of God.

In the hope that I might find a solution for my problem of death, I searched through the Bible. But when I was unwilling to come to Jesus Christ, I perished. On the days of my youthful vigor, my soul entered the abyss of perishing.

After the vision described above, my ardor for the world significantly cooled down. Even though my body was at work, my soul looked up to heaven. I was searching for salvation, while asking, "What shall I do to be saved from this life of perishing?"

Today I look back on my young life of death and perishing in the world, and give thanks to my God for His love. He looked on my wanderings and my troubles. In His kindness, He showed me that I was in the peril of perishing into hell in eternity. He warned me through the vision about my impending calamity and spoke to me to consider Jesus, the Savior. Nevertheless, I did not realize His warning at that time and went on my way in the world. All my sufferings and visions did not bring me to repentance from my sinful way. Still, I stubbornly rejected the word of God for my salvation. So my soul remained in the darkness of death. The days were the darkest days of my life.

Hell is the Destiny of Sinners

Let me warn you by the mercy of God that all sinners will perish through death. The unbelievers will perish without the life of God. Eternal life and heaven are far from those who are far from the God of life. The dead in sin will perish from the world of the living into the world of the dead, hell. The living dead will enter hell in eternity when they die physically. In the meantime, when the living dead plunge into the abyss of perishing, they will experience a living hell and cry out to the Lord God for help in their trouble, "Save us, O God!"

Summary and Application of Parts One and Two

We hope for a happy life. We wish our hearts to be filled with righteousness, love, peace, and joy. But what's happening to our lives? We see sin and death in our lives. We have tears from our eyes, wounds in our hearts, and pain and groaning in our souls.

We set out on our pilgrimage to heaven with hopes and dreams. But we could not enter heaven. We were afflicted with manifold troubles in the world, including captivity, poverty, and wilderness. We served our enemies in the lack of all things and entered the abyss of perishing. We were in distress.

How did we get here?

Because of our unbelief, we knew neither the Lord our God nor the way of life and heaven. We pursued eternal life and heaven all wrong. We attempted the pilgrimage to heaven along man's way, a wrong way. We looked for eternal life in the world, a wrong place. Our sinful ways led us to death. In the abyss of death, we perished from the life and glory of God and tasted death in a living hell.

Are you seeking life by the unbelieving, sinful way? You cannot find life on the path of death. You may say in your heart, "I do not believe in Jesus Christ, but I have peace. I am still at ease though I walk in my own way." But you do not yet know that you are lost in the world and are in danger of perishing. You just cannot see the darkness of death and do not realize the troubles in your soul.

Do not be deceived. There is a direct link between the ways of life and the conditions of life. The unbelieving way leads to death and adversity. There are many difficulties and troubles for everyone who does evil. The workers of sin will perish on the day of God's judgment. If you walk on the path of sin, you will stumble under the heavy burdens of death and fall into the abyss of darkness. There you will surely perish. I am the man who has seen all these evils. My soul had mountains of troubles. On the day when my soul was perishing into the abyss of death, I was in great distress.

You may wonder, "Is the terrible tragedy of perishing the end of human story? Can the perishing see good days?" In appearance, death looks to be the end of human journey. The grave seems to be the destination of man. But death and perishing are not the end of all things. God raises the dead. The Lord God saves the perishing.

Yes, there is hope—in God.

Hope in God for His help.

Seek the God of our salvation. There is the good news of God's salvation in Jesus Christ.

Why are you in despair? We have the Savior Jesus.

Part Three: The Way of God

6. Jesus Christ

Jesus Christ, the Word of God
God's Salvation Is Offered to the Perishing
People Would Not Believe in Jesus Christ

The Mystery of Jesus Christ

The Revelation of Jesus Christ
The Revelation of Jesus, the Christ, the Son of God
The Vision of God

The Work of God for Man
Overview
To Repent from Sinful, Perishing Ways to the Lord God
To Believe in Jesus Christ, the Son of God

Jesus Christ, the Word of God

God has spoken His word, the good news of Jesus Christ, to us. He performed many miracles and signs through Jesus and witnessed that Jesus is the Christ (God's anointed or appointed Savior of the world), the Son of God. Jesus Christ was almighty in deeds and words in the sight of all the people. He was crucified for our sins, buried, and raised from the dead on the third day. After appearing to many people, He was exalted to the right hand of God and has poured forth the Holy Spirit, the promised gift of God.

This is the word of God that we hear from the good news of Jesus Christ. The good news is that God saves us not according to our works, good or evil, but according to His grace in Jesus Christ. God's way of saving the perishing to eternal life is Jesus Christ.

God's Salvation Is Offered to the Perishing

God is calling all the peoples of the world to His salvation in Jesus Christ. In Jesus, sinners find the grace of God for the forgiveness of sin. Through the Christ, the blind receive sight. The captives are set free from all things. The poor are called to the riches of God's inheritance. The weak become strong in the strength of God's power, the lost are found, the dead are raised to life, and the perishing in hell are saved to heaven.

The salvation of God in Jesus Christ is for everyone, including Jews and Gentiles, the good and the evil, and the holiest people and the vilest sinners.

You are not like other sinners: murderers, adulterers, stealers, or liars. You have a religion, you were baptized with water, you read the Scriptures, you fast and pray, and you do acts of charity. Nevertheless, you know in your heart that you cannot enter the kingdom of God through your religion and your righteousness. Cease striving to look righteous and godly. Come to the Savior Jesus and receive the gift of God's righteousness by faith. Witnessing the miracles of God done to you and others, you believe Jesus Christ. God healed your sickness or disease in the name of Jesus. God helped you in your troubles. And you know that God is with Jesus and that He can perform miracles. If your faith rests on the miracles of God, listen to what the Lord Jesus says, "No one can enter the kingdom of God unless he is born of water and the Spirit." You must be washed by the Holy Spirit through Jesus Christ to enter the kingdom of God.

Are you searching for the way to God? Jesus said, "I am the way." Do you want to know the truth? Jesus is the truth. Come and behold the Son of God, full of glory and truth. Are you seeking the life of peace and joy? Come to Jesus Christ, and you will find eternal life. Come just as you are. You who have no good works can come to Him. The salvation of God is a free gift to everyone who believes in His Son, the Christ Jesus.

People Would Not Believe in Jesus Christ

The unbelievers ask for the signs of Jesus by saying, "Show me a sign from heaven, so that I may see the power of God and believe in Jesus Christ." Skeptics demand proofs of God's power for their faith.

As you know, Jesus performed many miracles. The miracles of Jesus are His signs showing as the Christ of God who saves the perishing to eternal life. Through the signs of Jesus, God has conspicuously displayed many convincing proofs for us to believe in the Christ of God. Jesus was clearly declared the Son of God with the power of God by His resurrection from the dead. The miracles of Jesus demonstrated unmistakable evidences of God's power in His works. The miraculous signs of Jesus manifested His glory as the Son of God. They are for us to behold the Son of God and believe in Him.

Yet most of the Jews did not believe in Jesus Christ. They expected their Messiah or Christ who would come like an almighty warrior and defeat all their enemies. (At the time of Jesus on the earth, the Roman Empire was the enemy of Israel.) They were hoping that Jesus was going to restore the kingdom of God to Israel on this earth. When they witnessed Jesus crucified, however, they could not see any signs of the divine power. All they saw was His suffering and death. Suffering is not the power of the world but a sign of weakness. Jesus had no the majestic glory of the Messiah that they should look on Him, but suffered the shameful death on a cross as a condemned criminal. A man hanging on the cross is not a blessed man but a cursed man to the Jews. The unbelieving Jews reviled Jesus hanging on the cross, saying in mockery, "Come down from the cross, if you are the Son of God. If you are the Savior of the world, save yourself, and we will believe in you." The proud, disbelieving Jews stumbled over Jesus Christ in their blindness. The way of God in Jesus Christ is righteous; sinners stumble in it.

The peoples of the nations search for the wisdom of God in the good news of Jesus Christ. But we proclaim, "Jesus who died on the cross is the Lord and Savior of the world." The wise people of the world would not accept the message of the cross of Jesus Christ; it is foolishness to them. The sufferings of the Savior are contrary to the wisdom of the world. His death nullifies all human wisdom. The word of the cross confounds the wise and they say in great perplexity, "How could the Savior of the world be crucified to death by the hands of men? It doesn't make sense." The death of the Savior is nonsense to them, and they would not believe in Him.

The noble people of the world despise the cross of Jesus Christ; it is the shameful things of the world. They see no pleasure in the painful, horrible death of Jesus. Blood, pains, and death are not the dignified things of the world. They turn their faces away from Jesus not to see Jesus suffering on the cross and stop up their ears not to hear the disgraceful things. The noble would not believe the shameful story. In fact, they are offended by the true way of the cross and take offense against the word of God with outright ridicule.

Furthermore, the virgin birth of Jesus is a scandal to the unbelievers. The message of the resurrection of Jesus is absurdity to them, and they would not believe it. They say, "There is no resurrection of the dead. How can the dead live again? It is unbelievable."

The Mystery of Jesus Christ

Jesus Christ is a mystery of God to the unbelievers. He is hidden from the wise people of the world. They have never heard or seen the amazing things of Jesus Christ, nor have they understood them. The Lord God has not given them ears to hear His word, nor eyes to see His glory, nor a heart to know who Jesus is. Their unbelieving hearts are hardened and senseless; the ears of their hearts are unable to hear. The eyes of their hearts are in darkness; they are unable to see. Consequently, they keep on hearing the good news of Jesus Christ but do not understand it. They keep on seeing the miracles of Jesus but do not perceive the glory of God in the Christ, the image of God. Whenever they hear the word of God, they are utterly bewildered with astonishment and continue in great perplexity.

On the first day when I was seeking the word of God at Capilano Canyon in Vancouver, I read about the birth of Jesus Christ in the Gospel according to Matthew in the Bible. The Bible said that a virgin

Mary gave birth to a son, Jesus. The word of God was unbelievable to me; I have never heard or seen such a thing. The virginal conception of Jesus without human father was impossible in my apprehension of things. When I pondered how this could be, my heart was greatly troubled at the word by the storm of doubts. I contemplated her body to understand the miracle and asked in deep perplexity, "How could this be possible, since she was a virgin? A virgin bore a son?" I could not understand this biological anomaly with my knowledge; it contradicted the ordered nature and was unnatural. The more I wrestled with it, the more baffling it got. Finally I concluded, "Impossible! It is nonsense!"

Do you understand the virgin birth of Jesus? As long as you contemplate the virgin Mary and her body in order to understand the miracle, you will not be able to comprehend it. It is indeed impossible for a virgin to conceive a baby by her own power. You cannot hope for the natural birth of a child from a virgin who knew no man. The conception of Jesus was brought about not by the flesh of the virgin Mary but by the almighty power of the Holy Spirit of God. The miracle of the virgin birth was the work of the supernatural power of God.

Do you still consider it incredible that the Creator God gave birth to a son through a virgin? Then, great is the mystery of Jesus Christ who came in the flesh of man to the world.

The intellectuals of the world find scientific problems in the miracles of Jesus, for example, the biological anomaly of the virgin birth, the medical anomaly of healing the sick without medication, the chemical anomaly of changing water into wine, and the physical anomaly of walking on water. They attempt to resolve such anomalies and ask in doubt, "How are these scientific anomalies possible?" Their difficulties over understanding the miracles of Jesus are in their inability to explain the things that their eyes have never seen and their hearts have never understood.

The miracles of Jesus are the works of God, which are beyond the natural wisdom and power. They are not the things of this world or of man and therefore are incomprehensible to human reason. We cannot explain the supernatural things with our natural, finite intelligence.

Therefore, if you look at the miracles of Jesus and ponder to comprehend them, the wonders of God will be inexplicable to your reason and troublesome in your sight. Doubts will arise in your heart. Your heart will be filled with the blinding darkness of unbelief; you will plunge into darkness.

There is no wonder why the intelligent people of the world cannot believe in Jesus Christ. The nearsighted by unbelief see the miracles of Jesus, but the spiritual blind cannot see His signs. The signs of Jesus are veiled to the eyes of their unbelieving hearts. As a result, they see only the miracles of Jesus Christ, not His signs manifesting the glory of the Christ and the Son of God. For instance, upon hearing about the work of Jesus healing the born blind in the Bible, John chapter 9, the unbelieving Jews saw the man healed by Jesus but could not see the sign of Jesus nor recognize the Son of God. If you are nearsighted by unbelief, you will see the healed man, clay, and Siloam. To understand how the blind man received sight, you will investigate the clay of the spittle and the pool of Siloam. But you know they have no power to open the eyes of the born blind and would not believe in Jesus Christ, the Son of God.

There is no need to explain or interpret the amazing events of Jesus. The will of God is for us to see the signs of Jesus beyond His miracles—that is, to behold the Son and the Christ of God and believe in Him. By faith, we understand Him and His works.

Now, let us take a simple eye examination to see if you are nearsighted and blind. Look at the cross of Jesus, not the one hanging on the church building or the one on the neck of a person as an accessory, but the one where the Son of God was lifted up high for the world to behold His glory and believe in Him.

What do you—can you—see?

You see the wooden cross and a righteous man called Jesus hanging on the cross in weakness and suffering death. But can you see the power and glory of God revealed through the Son of God? Can you see the truth and grace of God realized in Jesus Christ? Do you see the love of God for you?

If your answers are no, you are nearsighted and blind. The wonderful things of God in Jesus remain in a great mystery to you. They are beyond the range of your natural apprehension.

The nearsightedness and blindness of the unbelieving heart is also evidenced in hearing the good news of God's grace for sinners. Hearing the parable of "the prodigal son" in the Bible, Luke chapter 15, the unbelievers cannot see the father's grace for his returned son. Like the older son in the parable, while seeking justice for the younger brother who squandered his estate with loose living, the blinded by unbelief do not see the amazing grace of the father for the repented and returned sinner. All they can see is the unjust treatment of the father for his sons. They are angry about the injustice and are lost in the darkness of anger, and do not see the grace of God for sinners.

Look at the cross of Jesus Christ again. While seeing the man Jesus suffering on the wooden cross, the unbelievers cannot perceive the grace and truth of God revealed in Jesus. They do not see the love of God appeared for sinners, nor do they see God's righteousness revealed for sinners. They look at the blood and death of Jesus, but do not see the judgment of God revealed from heaven against their sins. For this reason, the intellectuals of the world cannot understand why the Savior of the world had to die for our sins and rise again from the dead in the power of God. The wisdom and power of God in Jesus Christ are in a mystery. All they see is the weakness and foolishness of God. They do not understand the great things of the cross.

Hearing the resurrection of Jesus from the dead, people look at the empty grave of Jesus, but the spiritual blind cannot see the risen Lord Jesus. They seek the risen Lord in the tomb, but He is not there. He rose from the dead. When God raised Jesus, they consider it incredible; they do not understand God's power of resurrection. A witness who has seen the risen Lord Jesus says to them, "Behold the Lord and Savior Jesus." They say, "Where is He? Show me."

Are you still asking for the signs of Jesus as the Son of God in order to see the power and glory of God and believe in Him? Hearing the message of the cross of Jesus, if you look at the visible things of His sufferings and death in weakness, you cannot believe in the Son of God. As long as you hang on your demand for the visible signs of

Jesus and use your own intellectual efforts to understand the good news of Jesus Christ, you will never come to know Him. Though the eyewitnesses of the risen Lord Jesus describe it to you, you will never understand the power and glory of God. If you are unwilling to come to the Lord, Jesus Christ will be ever a mystery to you.

On the other hand, the believers know what the good news of Jesus Christ is and what it can do. When the word of God is preached, it comes not only in word, but also in the kingdom, power, and glory of God. It is the power and wisdom of God for salvation to those who believe in Jesus Christ. God can raise the dead by the power of His Spirit; He can save the perishing in sin and death to eternal life.

The way of God in Jesus Christ transcends natural sight and is beyond human wisdom and understanding. It is hidden in the mystery of God. You study the Scriptures to know God but cannot come to know God through your wisdom. You have no idea about who Jesus really is. Jesus Christ is veiled in a mystery of God until you come into the presence of God and see His glory. The mystery of Jesus Christ can be known only by His revelation and to those who are enlightened by the light of His glory.

Therefore, our only hope is the self-revelation of God through His Son Jesus Christ. When you turn to the Lord, you will behold the glory of the Lord, know the Lord Jesus Christ, and believe in Him. In this case the saying "Seeing is believing." is true. The witnesses of the risen Lord Jesus believe not the unbelievable things of God in a mystery but the revealed and believable things of God.

Today if you hear the good news of Jesus Christ, do not look into your heart to understand them. If you do, you will see the darkness of doubts. Just turn your eyes to the Lord Jesus, and you will see the revelation of Jesus Christ.

The Revelation of Jesus Christ

The Revelation of Jesus, the Christ, the Son of God

The Son of God descended from heaven into the world and appeared in the flesh as the person Jesus. He was lifted up high on the cross and revealed His glory, so that we might turn to Him and see His glory. Behold the Son of God and see His eternal kingdom, power, and glory.

The mystery of godliness was veiled in God in the past, but now has been revealed by the appearing of Jesus Christ. God has revealed Himself; the invisible God became visible to us. The light of God's glory enlightens the eyes of the heart. In the sufferings of the Savior Jesus on the cross, God's grace for sinners has appeared. The love of God for us was manifested on the cross.

The blind (physical) cannot see the world or themselves. They cannot see the way of life in the dark and are in need of help from neighbors or assistive technology. Likewise, the unbelieving and blind (spiritual) dwelling in the darkness of death are helpless and hopeless in the world without God. Their only hope is the grace of God to be brought at the revelation of Jesus Christ. Hearing the good news of God's grace in Jesus Christ, they turn to the Lord and receive sight at the revelation of Jesus Christ.

The resurrection of Jesus Christ from the dead displayed the power of God. The almighty power of God has appeared, so that the world may know the greatness of His power raising the dead. Our Savior Jesus has shown us the way to enter life and heaven.

The eternal life of God was with God in heaven and now has been revealed to us through the good news of Jesus Christ. And we have seen the life with our eyes. The way into the presence of God has been unveiled through Jesus Christ. The presence of God is not far from us; He is very near us. The risen Lord Jesus has appeared to His people.

Turn to the Lord, and He will reveal Himself to you. The veil of darkness covering your unbelieving heart will be taken away and you will see the vision of God.

The Vision of God

The light of God's glory in Jesus Christ shined in our hearts in darkness. The eyes of our hearts were enlightened to see the vision of God. We beheld the glory of the Lord our God with our eyes and gained an insight into the mystery of Jesus Christ. The apostle John beheld the glory of Jesus as the Son of God. The risen Lord Jesus appeared to the apostle Paul on the way to Damascus and he saw the vision of God. He received the good news of God's grace through the revelation of Jesus, the Son and the Christ of God. John Newton, an evangelist and pastor in the eighteenth century, wrote about the amazing grace of God by saying, "I once was blind, but now I see." Fanny Crosby, a hymn writer in the nineteenth century, was blind (physically and spiritually). At a revival meeting, she saw the glory of the Lord and said, "My very soul was flooded with celestial light."

In the course of those days in 1976 when I was seeking God and His life, I became interested in public speaking. Hearing about the reputation of Billy Graham, I began to watch his evangelistic crusade on TV. I listened to his speaking not to hear the way of my salvation but to learn the art of speaking. Of course, I would not have watched the crusade if I knew he was a preacher of Jesus Christ. So I cared little for his message and examined his speaking by analyzing his speech. Many times—about twelve—I heard his speeches, but nothing of his message of Jesus Christ went into my closed heart. One evening he spoke about the healing of a leper in the Jordan River from the Bible, Second Kings chapter 5. The speaker made the comment that we have to look beyond the river to the One who made the miracle possible. Then he said something like this: "Look at the cross of Jesus. See God beyond the wooden cross. See the power and glory of God." So I turned my eyes to the cross and lifted up my gaze to heaven to see the God of glory.

Suddenly I fell into a trance and the vision of God appeared to me. I saw the heaven opened up and a great light from heaven shining on me, filling the whole world. When I beheld the glory of the Lord, I recognized Him and realized that I was standing in the presence of

God. At that moment I perished; the world and I disappeared. All was the glory of God.

The vision of God was so holy and awesome. The glorified Lord Jesus was exalted on high in heaven in His holiness. He had seen my sufferings and given heed to the cry of a poor sinner in the days of my distress. I was in the abyss of perishing. When I heard the message of the cross of Jesus, I turned to the Lord and beheld His majestic glory. His presence was there, revealing His eternal power and glory to me. Holy is the Lord our God! The risen Lord and Savior appeared to me. As the light of God's glory filled my soul, I saw the majestic splendor of Jesus and the greatness of His power. When I stood in the presence of God, I perceived my end. I, a sinner being short of the power and glory of God, perished in the presence of God. There was no place for the world or a sinner.

The mystery of Jesus Christ was made known to me through the revelation of the risen Lord Jesus. The light of God's glory enlightened the eyes of my heart, and I beheld the glory of the Son of God. The Holy Spirit of wisdom and revelation gave me the knowledge of God. The life of God has been manifested to me, and I have seen it with my eyes and received it with my heart.

Come to the Lord Jesus and see the vision of God for yourself. You will behold the glory of God if you turn your eyes on the Lord Jesus. Look intently at Him until His glory shines in your heart, and you will experience the power of God for salvation and believe in Him.

By the revelation and vision of Jesus Christ, we come to know the Lord God. We have seen the glory of the risen Lord Jesus with our eyes. We are eyewitnesses of the risen Lord and Savior; we know for sure that Jesus is the Christ, the Son of God.

The Work of God for Man

Overview

Now, what does God require from us for His salvation? What must we do to be saved from perishing to eternal life? What do we need to do to enter heaven?

The will of God is for us to repent and believe in Jesus the Christ, the Son of God. This is the work of God for us to have eternal life and enter heaven. To reach the destination of heaven, we do not need to try to ascend into heaven through our works of the laws of God or the Bible studies. Who can ascend into heaven? No one, except the One who came down from heaven. The Son of God came down into the world and ascended into heaven for us. Just repent and turn to the Lord. The Lord Jesus was lifted up high on the cross so that we might repent and believe through Him. Our Lord and Savior Jesus died for our sins, was buried, and rose from the dead for us. The good news of Jesus Christ is preached to save those who repent and believe. The message of the cross is proclaimed to us in order that we should repent from our sinful, perishing ways and believe in the risen Lord Jesus. The message of the resurrection of Jesus exhorts sinners to repent for the forgiveness of sins and believe in the Savior Jesus for eternal life.

Repenting and believing are not solely man's own works. A person with a depraved, ignorant heart cannot repent or believe in Christ Jesus by the person's own efforts. Apart from the Lord Jesus, the person can do nothing; the perishing person is helpless and hopeless without God. Conversely, we can do all things by the Holy Spirit through Jesus Christ. As the Holy Spirit reveals the life and glory of God in Jesus Christ to us, we are humbled in the presence of God to repent. Being enlightened by the light of the revelation of Jesus Christ, we see the errors of our ways and repent of our sins. Our realization about Jesus Christ and ourselves in the light leads us to repentance from our sinful ways. The grace and truth of God revealed through Jesus Christ lead us to faith. We repent and believe in a response to the revelation of Jesus Christ by the Holy Spirit. Job, an ancient man of many words in sufferings without understanding, was stilled before the God of creation. Having seen the vision of God with his eyes and his true self in the light of God's glory, he confessed his own insignificance and sinfulness. He became humbled before the sovereign Lord God and repented in dust and ashes. Peter was a Jew, a businessman in Galilee, and lately a disciple of Jesus. He stood tall before people. But one day when he stood before Jesus and recognized the Lord, he fell down to his knees before the Lord in prostrating humility and said, "Go away from me, Lord; I am a sinful man!" Beholding the Lord of power and glory, he saw his sinfulness and wretchedness. The apostle Paul once persecuted the Christians to destroy the faith in Jesus Christ, the Son of God. But when he encountered the risen Lord Jesus and saw the glory of God in Jesus, he repented his sin and believed in the Christ Jesus.

To Repent from Sinful, Perishing Ways to the Lord God

The word "repent", derived from the Greek word *metanoeo*, denotes to perceive after or change mind. It refers to turning the heart after having realized the mistakes made ignorantly in unbelief. To repent is to turn the heart from one's ways of sin and perishing to God for righteousness and life. The call to repent is to turn from man's way in the world to the way of God in Jesus Christ.

Hence, repentance is neither sorrow according to the flesh nor sorrow in the world, but the sorrow according to godliness. The sorrow of the flesh produces remorse, regrets, and tears. Worldly sorrow brings death and is bitter to the soul. Judas, one of the twelve disciples of Jesus, betrayed the Lord and sold Him for thirty pieces of silver. When he saw that Jesus was condemned, he realized that he sinned by betraying innocent blood. He felt great sorrow and the pain of regret and returned the money. In the sorrow of the flesh, he could not find the way to repentance and salvation. He was swept by self-blame and sank into despair. Thus he went away and hung himself, falling to destruction. In contrast, the sorrow according to the good news of Jesus Christ produces repentance, leading to salvation. Godly sorrow is a broken and contrite heart directed to God, bringing life and joy. It is sweet to the soul.

Repentance in Jesus Christ has the two aspects of turning from and to. One is for us to turn from our unrighteous ways and ungodly deeds. Isaiah was a man of God and a prophet of Israel. One day he entered the temple of God and saw the Lord exalted in His holiness. Then he cried, "I am ruined! For I am a man of unclean lips." In the light of God's glory, he saw he was ruined by his sin. In repentance, he turned from his sinful way to the Lord for the forgiveness of his sin.

Once we come into the presence of God and behold His power and glory, the secrets hidden in our hearts are disclosed in the light of His glory. In that moment, we attain the true knowledge of ourselves in relation to God. Those who came to know God confess the truth about themselves. Abraham, a father of faith, said, "I am nothing but dust and ashes." Paul, an apostle of God, cried, "What a wretched man I am!"

One comes to know oneself fully only in the light of God's revelation in Jesus Christ. The vision of God leads to the vision of man. To know God is to know man; to know the holy God is to know a sinner. In the reference to God's power and glory, one sees oneself in truth. The secrets of one's heart are brought to the light. All the hidden things that we have done in darkness are disclosed. The cross of Jesus Christ shows that we sinners are perishing in sin and death. Therefore we repent in humility.

During my vision of the risen Lord Jesus in 1976, my heart was filled with the knowledge of God. In the next moment, the Lord showed me my unbelieving ways and all my evil deeds in the world over the years. Through the fast-forwarded review of the past errors of my life, I watched my counsels in my darkened heart and my walks in the darkness of the world. He reminded me of my secret plans for life, my toil and struggle, and my adversity and sufferings. Things did not go the way I had planned. My life did not turn out the way I had wished. In fact, I was going the very opposite way—the way of sin and death. All the secrets hidden in my heart were disclosed in the light of God's presence. So I could not hide myself before the Lord God. My soul became completely bare and all the things that I had done were exposed by the light. As God played the video reviewing my life so far, I saw the true reality of me. I was not a man of self-adequacy but a man of weakness and foolishness, living a life of sin and death. I was not somebody with wisdom and power but a man of insignificance. I was nobody. The haughty man was humbled to nothing before the holy Lord. I was convicted with a deep sense of sin and guilt. Having left God out of my life, I had spent my life in various sins. I had gone far away from God and had done wicked things in the world. It was shown that I was perishing into the black darkness of death in my sinful ways in the world. Now my eyes saw the Lord of power and glory, and my sinfulness were made known to me. Then I loathed myself for my sinful ways and all my evil deeds. I was a man without God, having no hope in the world. I repented from my sinful ways of the world and turned to the Lord for His mercy.

As we see the truth revealed in the cross of Jesus, we are convicted of our perishing in our sin. We know we acted wickedly in unbelief and ignorance. We are overwhelmed by the conviction of sinfulness and humble ourselves before the Lord God. Our proud, hard hearts become broken and contrite. Becoming loosened from the bonds of wickedness, we do not justify ourselves but plead guilty of sinning against God. In repentance, we turn from our sinful, perishing way of man in the world.

The other aspect of repenting is turning to the Lord God for His help in His grace. Being aware of perishing in our sin and death, we the poor sinners readily repent and turn to God for His grace in Jesus Christ. In repentance, we turn our eyes to the Lord our Savior Jesus. The helpless and hopeless sinners come to God for His salvation. David, a king of Israel, sinned against God by committing adultery with Bathsheba. He came to the Lord with a broken and contrite heart and sought for His grace and salvation. While he was perishing in the pit of death under the sea, Jonah, a prophet of Israel, repented and turned toward the holy temple of God and cried to the Lord for help.

The call of repentance is that we should stop striving to be righteous before God. Self-righteous people believe that they do not need to repent. When they look at their own righteousness and good works, they trust in themselves that they are righteous. In their own estimation, they stand tall and clean before God. And they say, "I'm a good man and need no repentance." They are offended when they are told to repent. They do not realize the true conditions of their souls until they come into the presence of God. Simply repent and turn to the Lord and Savior Jesus for the righteousness of God.

Repentance is for sinners. One parable of Jesus tells of a tax-gatherer who loved money and did evils to others. When he sensed his sin and guilt, he felt sorrow and grief in his broken heart before the holy God. But the poor and afflicted sinner could not put trust in him. He was so poor and broken that he had nothing to offer to buy his soul. Without God's mercy, he was hopeless in the world. And he turned to God and pleaded for His mercy to save him from the depth of distress, "God, have mercy on me, a sinner." God justified the man of godly sorrow. The man went back to his home with peace and joy.

Jesus Christ was lifted up on the cross so that we may repent and turn our hearts to the Lord and Savior. Everyone who turns to the Lord Jesus and fixes one's hope completely on the grace of God will find it at the revelation of Jesus Christ.

To repent is to return home through Jesus Christ. Those who turned to the world and went far away from God repent and return home for life. The lost in sin and death come to the Father in heaven for the gift of eternal life. God the Father is gracious and welcomes repentant and returning sinners. Therefore, the call to repentance is a message of hope. The hungry and thirsty will be satisfied with the heavenly things and delight themselves in abundance. The dead will come to life—that is, eternal life. This is why repenting is a pleasant and joyful experience. The repentance of one sinner brings joy to God, the angels, and saints.

Why are you wandering in the world far from home? Your soul is longing for home. Deep down in your heart is hunger for righteousness, love, peace, and joy. Oh, repent and come home. The Father is waiting for you to come home for all things in abundance. Do not fear Him. You have sinned, but He is gracious. He will accept you as His son or daughter in the name of His Son, our Savior Jesus. Consider your ways and turn to the Lord and Savior Jesus. Dying with hunger in a distant country and coming to his senses, the prodigal son in the parable of Jesus repented and returned to his father for life.

Our Savior Jesus opened the way for us to come to God by His death and resurrection. The good news of God is calling us to repent and come back to the Father in heaven for salvation. Hearing the call of God in the name of Jesus, the poor and afflicted forsake their evil ways and deeds in the world and come to the Lord God for His grace. One of the criminals who were crucified with Jesus repented his sin and turned to the Lord for His kingdom by saying, "Jesus, remember me when you come into your kingdom." Jesus said to the repenting man, "Today you will be with me in paradise."

You can come to the Lord God. If you should say in your heart, "My sins are too great. How can I come to Him?" Do not fear. He does not despise a repenting heart. Repentant sinners find the abounding grace of God in Jesus Christ. He will forgive you. Jesus Christ came into the world not to condemn sinners but to save them. He came to call sinners to repent and live. The good news of God assures us that God will receive us graciously. The grace of God is more abundant than your sins. The Lord does not require from you offerings and sacrifices for your sin. The Lord and Savior Jesus already paid for you. Just turn to the Lord for His grace. The Lord your God is waiting for you. Arise, come and see the salvation of God. If you come, you will find ready help from the Lord and Savior.

But if you do not repent with the stubbornness of your unbelieving heart, you will continue on your way to destruction. Refusing to repent means to hold fast to your sinful way of death. When you hide your sins, your guilt will be heavy on you. You will not prosper but perish in your sin and death.

Why should you perish? Repent and live. There is the Savior Jesus. Look to the Savior and live. Oh, don't you want to repent and turn to the Savior Jesus for the forgiveness of your sins? The work of repenting is easy and simple. Repenting is as easy as looking—looking up to the Lord and Savior Jesus who was lifted up on the cross. If you look, you will live.

Through the good news of Jesus Christ, God has promised the forgiveness of sins and the gift of the Holy Spirit. Give heed to the word of God for salvation. Repent and turn to the Lord. Behold the Son of God, and you will believe in Jesus Christ, the Son of God.

To Believe in Jesus Christ, the Son of God

The message of God's grace in Jesus Christ is preached to save those who behold the Son of God and believe in Him. The beholder of the glory of God is convinced to believe in Him. Through the revelation of Jesus Christ, we have received faith toward God. So the work of believing in Jesus Christ is not the heavy burden of believing the unseen, unbelievable things of God. Beholding the Lord in His glory, we are fully convicted by the truth to believe in the Son of God. Believing the seen, believable things of God is easy and comfortable.

The good news of Jesus Christ came to us in the Holy Spirit and with the full assurance and conviction of faith. Having seen the life and glory of God, our hearts are fully assured of the things that God promised and we hoped for. We are convicted to believe the truth of Jesus Christ. By the works of the Holy Spirit in our hearts, Jesus Christ became our faith and hope.

Upon hearing the hope in Jesus Christ about the promised and unseen things of God, we believe in hope beyond the seen things of the world. As the Holy Spirit discloses the things of God to us, we leave behind all definite thoughts and apparent evidences and surrender ourselves to the inexpressible longing for the things of God, which are unattainable in the world.

On the day in 1976 when I saw the vision of God and the light of God's glory filled my soul, all the darkness of my doubts disappeared. The good news of Jesus Christ came to me in the Holy Spirit and with the full assurance and conviction of faith. I received the faith in Jesus Christ through the revelation of Jesus Christ. My insight into the mystery of Christ Jesus led my soul to believe in the Lord and Savior Jesus. The grace of God revealed on the cross fully assured me to believe in the Lord Jesus. I was fully convicted to know my God and myself in truth. Jesus, who died on the cross, is our God and Savior. I came to know that I am a sinner perishing in my sin. I fixed my hope of salvation on the grace of God brought to me at the revelation of Jesus Christ.

The faith we have received through Jesus Christ has its knowledge and its works.

The Knowledge of Faith

Through the revelation of Jesus Christ and our vision of God's glory, we believe and know Jesus, the Christ and the Son of God. In the light of the glory of God in Jesus, we come to the knowledge of the Lord God. So our faith in Jesus Christ is not blind faith but enlightened faith. God has shone His light in our hearts to give the knowledge of His glory in Jesus Christ. The eyes of the believing heart are enlightened to see the glory of the Lord, the riches of His life, and the greatness of His power. Our faith in Jesus Christ is based on our personal knowledge of God. The knowledge of God makes us believe not in ourselves but in the God of eternal power and glory.

Christian faith is gained not through the creeds or statements of faith written by men but by the power of God for salvation. This is because God saves us by the Holy Spirit through Jesus Christ. Experiencing the salvation of God, we know that Jesus is the Lord our God who has saved us from death and perishing. We know by personal experience what the word of God can do to those who believe—that is, God saves us by the wonders of God. Therefore our faith is the full assurance and conviction in Jesus Christ. With the full assurance of faith, we know that we have eternal life.

The Works of Faith

The knowledge of faith produces the works of faith. Our full conviction about Jesus Christ works it out in our practice of faith. The living faith in our hearts is expressed in our works of faith. The faith in Jesus Christ works in trust and obedience.

We have beheld the eternal power and glory of God in Jesus Christ. The vision of God has convinced our hearts to trust such a God. The revelation of Jesus Christ in the fullness of grace and truth has led us to trust in the grace of God and obey the truth of God with all our hearts and with all our lives.

Hearing the good news of God's grace for sinners, poor sinners having nothing to offer to God for His favor simply trust in His grace revealed in the cross of the Savior Jesus. We trust in the God who is able to raise the dead with the power of resurrection.

Our faith in Jesus Christ is actively expressed in obedience to the truth. We know that the word of God is the truth and take the word of God fully in our hearts and obey the will of God completely. Beholding the truth of God manifested in Jesus Christ, we have obeyed it. In the obedience of faith, we have surrendered ourselves to the Lord and submitted ourselves to the grace and truth of God.

Fully convicted by my vision of God on the day of my salvation, I have trusted in the Lord and Savior to deliver me from my troubles. In the obedience of faith, I have committed myself to my Lord and Savior in complete surrender and eagerly received the grace of God in Jesus Christ.

When we repent and believe in a response to the word of God, Jesus Christ, God saves us by the wonderful works of the Holy Spirit through Jesus Christ.

7. God's Works to the Believer

Washing of Recreation and Renewal
Washing by the Holy Spirit
Recreating and Renewing
Giving the Holy Spirit

Sanctifying to the Lord God
Sanctifying by the Holy Spirit
Glorifying to the Glory of the Lord God

The good news of Jesus Christ comes to the believer not only in the word of God but also in the power of God. God saves everyone who believes in Jesus Christ by the washing of recreation and renewal by the Holy Spirit and by sanctifying to the Lord God. The believers experience the wonders of God's salvation.

Washing of Recreation and Renewal

Washing by the Holy Spirit

God pours out His promised Spirit on the believer abundantly through His Son, Jesus Christ. And the Lord Jesus baptizes (dips, overwhelms, or washes) the believer by the Holy Spirit.

The Holy Spirit came on us like the shower and performed the washing of God. As the spring shower washes nature and renews life, so does the Holy Spirit. The shower of the Holy Spirit washed us and renewed our lives. All our filthiness and idols were cleansed by the washing of the Holy Spirit. He purified our hearts from the evil conscience of our sins and evil works, and washed our bodies from all the defilement of unrighteousness and ungodliness. We the defiled by the world and sin became clean by the washing of the Holy Spirit. All our sins were washed away and our sin was forgiven; God remembers our sin no more.

Now we are clean before God. Our hearts are pure and our bodies are free from the stains of the world and the defilement of sin. God made us whole and we are perfect. We have the righteousness of God and have a good conscience before the Lord God. We have no guilt in life or worries about God's condemnation. And we have confidence to enter the holy place of God, and stand in the presence of His glory with great joy.

Recreating and Renewing

Through the baptism into Jesus Christ by the Holy Spirit, God recreated and renewed us in the likeness of God according to His image and glory. The Holy Spirit recreated us by baptizing us into the death, burial, and resurrection of Jesus Christ. We died into the death of Jesus Christ, were buried under the grace of God, and rose by the Holy Spirit as new creations.

At the moment of the baptism of the Holy Spirit, we were changed through death and resurrection into the same glory of God. The old people of sin and death died and the new people of righteousness and holiness rose from the dead. The new children of God were born by the Holy Spirit; we became the children of God. We who had been born of the flesh were reborn as the people of God. The natural people from earth were raised to the spiritual people from heaven. Now we have new hearts and are the new people of God for the new life in the Lord Jesus.

Who needs the recreation and renewal by the Holy Spirit? If you are a person born of the flesh without the new creation of God, you need it. You wish to stand in the presence of God, but God seems so far away? Then, you need it too.

When we are baptized by the Holy Spirit through Jesus Christ, God gives us the promised gift of the Holy Spirit.

Giving the Holy Spirit

On the day of my salvation in 1976 when I received the grace of God in Jesus Christ by faith, God poured out His Spirit on me. The Holy Spirit came to me abundantly and overwhelmed me in the power of God. He washed away my sins, recreated me, and renewed my heart and life. The Holy Spirit of love melted my cold and hard heart as the warm air of spring melts the frozen land. My insides freely ran like a rustling stream in the spring after the shower. My soul was washed away from an evil conscience and my body from the defilement of sin. I became clean. All my burdens of sin and death were lifted at that moment. I felt a release from the bondage of foreign powers. I was set free from all things and felt like flying. The Holy Spirit of life renewed my heart. My stubborn and hard heart like stone became soft and tender like the flesh of a newborn baby. All the wounds and scars within me were healed and I became whole. My heartland of wilderness was transformed into the paradise of God. Instead of thorns and thistles, the fruit of life filled my heartland.

As I received the Holy Spirit through Jesus Christ, my soul was filled with the life of God. The Spirit of God satisfied my thirsty soul with the living water of heaven and filled my hungry soul with the good things of heaven. The life of God overflowed in my soul, and I greatly rejoiced in the abundance of all things. I have never experienced the heavenly ecstasy of such great peace and joy in my soul before. What a wonderful experience it was! It was heaven.

When I woke up from the trance (begun with my first vision of God described in chapter 6), my body was strangely warm. My face was burning and my cheeks were hot. Holding my cheeks in my hands, I rose from the armchair where I was reclining to watch a televised evangelistic crusade. I leaped for joy and ran along the hallway leading to the master bedroom to look for someone and tell about what had just happened to me. Finally, reaching the kitchen, I found somebody standing. It was my wife. I said to her, "Honey, something wonderful happened to me tonight." Tears filled her eyes—this time out of joy. She knew the salvation of God finally came to me.

At the time, I did not understand what had happened to me. In a moment, what a change had taken place in me! The experience was inexpressible with words. The newness, the love, the peace, and the joy were too amazing for me. The wonders of God done to me surpassed all my comprehension. All I knew was something wonderful happened to me. And I was so eager to tell somebody about it.

The day proved to be a turning point in my pilgrimage to heaven. On that day, the Lord my God did His wonders to me. He saved me by the washing of recreation and renewal by the Holy Spirit through Jesus Christ. I came to know the salvation of God by experiencing the forgiveness of my sin and the life of God. I was once perishing in my sin and death, but was raised to the life of God by the Holy Spirit. I was a man of weakness and dishonor, but God transformed me into His power and glory. God changed me completely and made me a new person with a new heart. I was born of God to be His son with the Holy Spirit.

Ever since the Holy Spirit came to me, times of renewing have come to me. I have begun the new life of holiness and righteousness. God has made all things new by His power. As the Holy Spirit of life has filled my soul, all of my former foolish desires and bad habits disappeared. Now I have new desires and good habits of the things of the Holy Spirit, resulting in life and peace.

Spring has arrived to me with the showers of God's grace and the warm breezes of the Holy Spirit. The grace of God flows in my soul like a mighty river renewing my life. As the Lord renews my body and soul, my life is refreshed in His life and glory.

God bestowed His Spirit within us who had been purified by the Holy Spirit. Now we have eternal life. The Holy Spirit waters our souls with the living water of God and gives us the eternal life of love, peace, and joy. Our hearts filled with the Holy Spirit overflow with life. The love of God flows from the purified heart for God and neighbors. We delight ourselves in the abundance of life. In the presence of God, we are renewed according to the image of God and are all transformed into the same image of glory. We have a new life and a new beginning in Christ Jesus. We walk in the newness of the Holy Spirit.

God put the robe of His righteousness on us, the purified by the Holy Spirit; we are clothed with the holy attire of God's glory. The shame of our nakedness is no longer revealed and we are holy and blameless. We are not ashamed before holy God and righteous people and stand in the presence of God joyfully.

The conversion by the Spirit of God is not the changes made by personal development and renovation. Nor is it a temporary, strange, emotional manifestation. The change we experienced is rebirth by the Holy Spirit. The newness is the recreation and renewal by the power of God. It is the new creation of God by the Holy Spirit through the baptism of death, burial, and resurrection with Jesus Christ. God changes us totally in our hearts and lives, and brings the complete changes that we could not do because of our weakness. He changes our personalities and all the areas of our lives—including, home, work, and community.

To obtain the change by the resurrection from the dead, one must die with Jesus Christ by faith. The believer dies with Jesus Christ and rises with Him to the resurrection by the Holy Spirit. The person born of the flesh is recreated and renewed to a new person born of the Holy Spirit through Jesus Christ.

People ask, "How does a living person die and is raised to life again?" Look at nature. When we sow a living grain of wheat, it dies in the ground and is raised as a wheat plant with a new body and life. So is the resurrection of the dead. When we are baptized by the Holy Spirit into the death of Jesus Christ and die with the Lord by faith, God raises us with the Lord to a new body and life. The Holy Spirit who raised Jesus from the dead revives us from the dead. In the likeness of His death and resurrection, we die to sin and rise from the dead to the eternal life in Jesus Christ.

You may inquire, "How can a person of sin and dishonor be changed into a person of life and glory?" The body and life of a wheat grain are changed by death and resurrection into the body and life of a wheat plant. So is everyone who is raised from the dead by the Holy Spirit. A natural person of death and wretchedness is transformed by the Spirit of God into a spiritual person of life and glory.

You can read books about swimming, but until you jump into water, you really have no idea about what it is like. So is with the Holy Spirit. Through the forgiveness of your sin and the newness of your life in the Holy Spirit, you know God's grace and salvation.

Sanctifying to the Lord God

Sanctifying by the Holy Spirit

As the Holy Spirit sanctifies us to the Lord God for His glory, we are separated from the world and sin to God and holiness. We are set apart for a holy ministry to stand before the Lord God and serve Him gladly. In the presence of God, we love and worship Him by the Holy Spirit through Jesus Christ.

God continues to work within me by the Holy Spirit through Jesus Christ after my salvation. As the Holy Spirit sanctifies me to the Lord my God, I devote myself as a sacrifice to the Lord. I continually devote myself to worship, to prayers, and to the word of God. Having tasted the grace of God, I long for the word of God with great appetite. The Lord nourishes me with the word of God to grow up into Himself.

In addition, I discipline myself for life and godliness day and night. Above all, I fix my eyes on the Lord Jesus to keep looking to Him, not to look at the other way to the world. Every time I behold the glory of the Lord, I enter the presence of God. There I continue to praise the Lord and give thanks to Him for His salvation in His grace. I am ready to do good works to others for the glory of God. Over the years, God has brought drastic changes to my personality and all aspects of my life. The Lord has caused me to grow up to a mature man.

Even after many years of God's works in me and my works by faith, I have not yet reached the goal of man—that is, to be like God. There is still a ceaseless striving after the perfection of God. But now I pursue it by the faith and hope in the Lord our Savior Jesus. My maturity is much nearer to the fullness of Jesus Christ than when I first believed.

As the Holy Spirit consecrates us wholeheartedly to be holy to the Lord God, the glory of God fills our souls. His glory is our glory. We are being transformed into the image and likeness of God in all glory.

Glorifying to the Glory of the Lord God

God calls us into His life and glory through the good news of Jesus Christ. The purpose and grace of God is for us to be holy and perfect like Him. He saves us by the washing, sanctifying, and glorifying works of the Holy Spirit through Jesus Christ. And God fills our souls with His life and glory. When we are glorified to the image and glory of God, we know the good, perfect will of God for us.

Praises and thanksgivings be to God through our Lord and Savior Jesus! We cried for help out of our troubles to the Lord our God. He listened to our prayers and saved us in His grace. To the God of our salvation be honor and glory. The eternal kingdom, power, and glory belong to the Lord our God.

Part Four: The Life in Christ Jesus

God saves the believers in the Christ Jesus by delivering them from captivity to freedom and then giving them the promised life in Christ Jesus. The life of freedom will be described in chapter 8 and the other aspects of the life will be portrayed in chapters 9 and 10.

We the believers have already received the life of God through Jesus Christ and are enjoying it. But we cannot explain the life in detail. First, it is eternal and heavenly and therefore transcends complete description with expressions. Second, our present experiences of eternal life are only a foretaste of what we shall experience it in the fullness of eternity in heaven. Moreover, its detailed portrayal is beyond my purpose. I write this book for you to believe in Jesus the Christ, the Son of God and experience the heavenly life for yourself. Therefore, the following three chapters sketch some of my experiences of the life in the Lord Jesus to show what the Christian life is like. With the help of the Holy Spirit, we shall look at the life focused separately with the Christian freedom, the riches of God's life, and the paradise of God.

8. Freedom

The Meaning of Christian Freedom
Deliverance from Sin and Death
Liberation from the Things of the World
Freedom from Self

The Means of Christian Freedom
Through the Death and Resurrection of Jesus Christ
By the Power of the Holy Spirit

The Objectives of Christian Freedom
To Love, Worship, and Serve the Lord Our God
To Love and Serve Our Neighbors
To Live Godly and Righteously

The Meaning of Christian freedom

Christian freedom is not of the world: it is not political, personal, or financial freedom. The people of God in some countries are politically ruled by foreign powers, yet they enjoy the freedom of God's kingdom. Some Christians are imprisoned for their faith; however, their spirits are free to pray for their persecutors. Some are poor in earthly things but freely make others rich with heavenly things. Nor is it the freedom of sinners in the flesh.

Christian freedom means the freedom in the Holy Spirit—that is, the spiritual freedom of the righteous people by faith in Jesus Christ. It is a freedom in the purified heart. Christians were delivered from all things, under which they had been in captivity.

Deliverance from Sin and Death

We were once enslaved to sin in the flesh and spent our lives in sins, and were condemned to death. But when the grace of God appeared in our Savior Jesus Christ, God delivered us from our captivity to sin and death. The Lord our Savior set us free from the bondage of our enemies to the freedom of the children of God.

We still live in the flesh, but we are not of the flesh. We were weak through the flesh, but now we are strong in the strength of God's power. The people of God with the Holy Spirit boldly say no to sin with the authority and power of the Lord. We no longer have obligation to obey sin or to live according to fleshly lusts and pleasures. We do not live in sin: we of the Holy Spirit live a righteous life free from sin. God gives us the victory over death.

Liberation from the Things of the World

There is bondage in the world, but there is liberty in the Holy Spirit of God. We were formerly in bondage to the worldly powers, but our God freed us from the old servitude. God delivered us from the dominion of Satan to the Lord our God. Our Savior Jesus liberated us from the yoke of slavery under the gods of the world, such as money, power, fame, and pleasures. We were also freed from all the burdens of the world—namely, the needs of earthly things and the worries of the world. The Lord our God supplies all our needs for godliness and life according to His riches. Furthermore, the Holy Spirit made us free from all the old masters of earthly things, including television, computer, hobby, tobacco, and alcohol.

We once lived in subjection to the elements of the world: the laws, customs, and traditions of men; the rudimentary knowledge of theology, philosophy, and science; and the morality and ethics of society, worldly religions, and superstitions. When our God saved us by His grace, He delivered us from all the constraints of the elements to live freely as His sons and daughters. God released us from the bounds and restrictions imposed by the elementary principles of the world.

There is no condemnation to us who were delivered from the law of God to the grace of God in Jesus Christ. We were released from the burdens of guilt and condemnation in the Law. We have no worries about the judgments of God and are free from the fear of death.

Freedom from the law of God does not mean that Christians are discharged from the obligation of the Law. We know that the Law is the will of God. The Law is righteous and good. Having been released from the bondage of the Law, we keep the Law not according to the letter of the Law but fulfill it by the freedom of the Holy Spirit. We serve God not as the slaves of the Law but as the children of God. The children of God love God the Father and liberally go beyond the letter of the Law to do the will of God with the Holy Spirit of love. Thus, we fulfill the Law by the Holy Spirit.

Freedom from Self

The Lord Jesus set us free from ourselves to love and serve others. We no longer live for ourselves but for the Lord our God and our neighbors. We do not merely seek our own personal lives, interests, and rights, but also those of our neighbors. Paul, an apostle of Jesus Christ, was a free man in the Holy Spirit and did not consider his own life as precious to himself. He was free to surrender himself to the will of God, even his own life if needed for the glory of the Lord and his neighbors.

The Means of Christian freedom

Through the Death and Resurrection of Jesus Christ

Christian freedom is obtained through the death and resurrection of Jesus Christ. His death on the cross broke the bond binding us to our foreign rulers, sin and the world's powers. Our old rulers no longer have power over us. (Death breaks the bond between a subject and the subject's ruler; the ruler has no power over the dead.) When we died with Jesus Christ by faith, all the foreign rulers in the flesh and in the world lost their grips on us. We the dead are not tempted by them, or respond to them. We rose with Jesus Christ to the new life of freedom through His resurrection.

On the day of my salvation, I was baptized into Jesus Christ by the Holy Spirit to die and rise with my Savior Jesus to the life of freedom. Now I practice my death and resurrection every day. I die and rise daily to live freely. I am dead with Jesus, but I live freely by the power of His resurrection. My death with Jesus Christ is my triumph and my freedom. When I die in the Lord, I can do all things with the authority and power of the Lord God. I am weak in the flesh, but I am strong with the Holy Spirit; I am poor in the world, but I am rich with God's inheritance; and I am afflicted in the body, but I am comforted by my God. I am free from want, for the Lord is my satisfaction. I am a son of God and am free from fear.

This is the message of the cross and resurrection of Jesus Christ—the message of liberation from self, sin, and the world.

By the Power of the Holy Spirit

Man of the flesh cannot attain Christian freedom. Through the weakness of the flesh, we cannot do the things of God as we please. But we can do all things by the power of the Holy Spirit. Through Jesus Christ, God redeemed us the slaves of sin to be His children. He bestowed the gift of the Holy Spirit on His children. We have the freedom in the Holy Spirit. The children of God are truly free.

Thanks be to God through Jesus Christ for the freedom in the Holy Spirit! He set me free from all things that had held me in captivity throughout my young years. Gaining the Holy Spirit, I lost the pleasures of the flesh and the desires for the things of the world. It was easy and comfortable for me to quit drinking, smoking, sinning, and doing other harmful habits and shameful lifestyles. Now I am a stranger to the things of the past.

The Objectives of Christian freedom

What is the will of God for the freedom found in Jesus Christ? What do we do with our freedom in the Holy Spirit?

Christian liberty is neither the permission for undisciplined living in the world nor the opportunity to live as we please. It is not the freedom of speech and expression to hurt others. Nor is it a license to break the law of God. Rather, it is the freedom to live according to the will of God. We use our freedom in the Holy Spirit to love and serve the Lord our God and our neighbors and to live godly and righteously.

To Love, Worship, and Serve the Lord our God

When I obeyed the truth of Jesus Christ, the Lord purified my heart to love God with all my heart and with all my life. My heart is pure with loving the Lord my God only and my life is simple with serving the Lord only. The Holy Spirit sanctifies me to be holy to the Lord and I devote myself to the ministry for the glory of the Lord God. Truly, the Lord is the worthy object I live for.

The following Sunday after the day of my salvation in 1976, I joined the Korean Baptist Church in Vancouver to serve the Lord. Soon after, I was baptized with water at the church. As an eyewitness of the divine glory of Jesus, I began to proclaim that Jesus is the Christ, the Son of God.

Then, my pilgrimage of faith started. I visited several churches in Vancouver in my search of a church that would satisfy my hunger for the word of God. The babe in Christ longed for the pure milk of heaven. After many churches, the Lord eventually led me to Faith Baptist Church in Vancouver. I served the Lord as a deacon at the church. To minister to the glory of God, I devoted the early hours of every morning, entered the holy place of God, and served the Lord with love and worship.

At one point in my earlier search for eternal life, I wished for just seven days of peace and joy. Now I have received the life of God in Jesus Christ. My Lord gave me far more than I had wished for. Realizing that the Lord made me an heir of eternal life in the present time and in eternity, I desired to live the rest of my life in the body no longer for myself but for the Lord and Savior who died and rose for me to have eternal life. My heart's desire was to dedicate myself to the Lord as a sacrifice for His service. For me to live was to glorify the Lord my God.

By the summer of 1982, I knew God had called me to minister to His glory as a pastor in His church. My calling to the pastoral ministry was sensed in three ways: First, the Spirit of God sanctified me to minister to the Lord our God. I had confidence to enter the holy presence of God with a true heart full of assurance of faith in Jesus Christ. I continually entered the presence of God and offered up the spiritual sacrifices of praise, thanksgiving, and good works to Him. I considered my life and my professional career as nothing in order to serve the Lord.

Second, I had a strong sense of obligation and an eager desire to proclaim the gospel of God's grace to all people. God inspired me to have deep compassion for the souls in need of the word of God. My heart was burdened for the lost in the world who were helplessly perishing in sin and death. I knew from my own experience what they were going through in their lives. Even though they were well learned in the things of the world and professed to be wise, they did not know that they were blind. They saw the glory of the visible world but could not see the glory of the Lord God of the world. They were misguided by the world and were perishing in their sin and death. I knew that they needed to hear the gospel of Jesus Christ. They need their sins forgiven, freedom from the bondage of sin, and a new life in Christ. My compassion for the unsaved souls compelled me to proclaim the gospel of hope. Additionally, when I saw the believers hungry for the word of God, I was eager to show them the way of spiritual growth and how they could become transformed into the glory of the Lord.

Third, many pastors and believers recognized my spiritual gifts as I served the Lord in the churches in Vancouver, and encouraged me to go into the ministry as a pastor.

Thus, I aspired to serve the Lord our God as a pastor full-time. My wife was about to find out that the Lord granted her far more than she had long been praying for. It was her turn to struggle with the material sacrifice required for the pastoral ministry. Knowing the financial hardships that the pastors of immigrants' churches face, she reasoned to me, "You don't have to be a pastor to serve the Lord. You can serve the church with generous donations and active ministries."

One year later, one day when I talked about the calling of God again, she entered her closet and prayed to the Lord. "If the Lord will use him as a pastor, I can do without material things." She told me, "No matter how tough it will be, I will go with you. Wherever you go, I will go with you. Where you live, I will live. The Lord has trained me to get by with humble means through the Korean War and by having lived in poverty in my young years as a refugee."

Now that our desires for worldly things were gone, we were free to live for the Lord our God. I freely left my professional career and business behind and followed the Lord for His service.

In September 1983 when I was forty-one, I began equipping myself at Northwest Baptist Theological Seminary in Vancouver. There I completed the course of Master of Divinity in two years. The call of God to the pastoral ministry that I sensed during my early life of salvation was confirmed in my heart while I was attending the seminary and ministering to the Lord and His people.

When I turned my eyes to Toronto, Ontario for the gospel in October 1985, I saw my children in school and heard a snowstorm on the way. Our friends suggested waiting for a better time, perhaps until the following year, but I was so eager to preach the gospel to the people in Toronto.

The next day after my seminary graduation, without waiting to raise financial support, we left Vancouver to go to Toronto. We were determined to give all that we had, even our life savings. With only an address, 24 Holmes Avenue, Willowdale, Ontario, as a destination, we set out on our journey to Toronto. We had a kindred feeling with Abraham, who went out at God's call "even though he did not know where he was going." We passed through the Canadian Rockies, the prairies of Alberta, Saskatchewan, and Manitoba, and the mountains of Northern Ontario in a rented one-ton truck with our three daughters (aged ten, eight, and six) and all our worldly possessions. The trip across the western Canada took us six days.

When we arrived at our destination and opened the milk box at the rented house, we found that the Lord had already made up the exact amount of the savings we offered to Him for our trip through the monetary gifts of His generous people. Again, we learned to fear the Lord our God and knelt down in the living room of the house and worshiped Him.

It took us a month to settle in the old, filthy house. I preached the gospel about the kingdom of God and Jesus Christ, and planted a church from scratch for the glory of God. The Lord gave me the grace and freedom to serve Him for the works of evangelizing the world and edifying His church. In the power of the Holy Spirit, I declared the way of salvation in Jesus Christ to the people in Toronto and beyond, and as far as Boston, Massachusetts, and Gainesville, Florida.

As a minister of God's grace, I endured the long, hard labors of going out at eleven o'clock in the evening to serve the storeowners who close their stores at that time. In many sleepless nights, I visited hospitals to care for the victims of family violence and those suffering from trauma. I prayed for the sick, comforted the afflicted, and cared for the dying. Through the hardships of concerns, heartbreaks, and sufferings for the church of God, I continually offered up sanctified people to God.

After eight years of ministry in Toronto, I aspired to move to a city in the United States for the gospel, but the Lord did not permit it. Instead, the Spirit of the Lord called me to serve a church in Edmonton, Alberta.

The calling of God meant great sacrifices for my family. We had been at our house for eight years and were quite settled. My wife had to lose all the comfort and security of her job, friends, and the familiar patterns of life. My children had to leave their friends and change their academic plans. Since grade-school systems and curriculums in the provinces of Ontario and Alberta were different, they faced the pains of being uprooted from the establishment in Ontario. The people around us objected to the idea of moving the family at this time.

By faith, however, we obeyed the call of God and moved to Edmonton in October 1993. Throughout our journey of four days on the road, worship songs for God filled our hearts and our car, and we followed the glory of God in heaven. My soul soared high into the sky and entered the heaven.

Immediately I preached the gospel of Jesus Christ to the people in Edmonton and shepherded the flock of God. A few persons opposed my preaching, hardened their hearts, and disobeyed the word of God. They said to me, "You must not preach the gospel of Jesus Christ to us. We hate the message of the cross. Speak to us with comforting words for the hardships of immigrants." But I continued to proclaim the gospel of God's grace to save their souls. Filled with indignation at my preaching, they rose up against me after the worship service that Sunday. There was a severe commotion in the basement of the church. The Lord was with me and delivered me from the danger of violence.

In the midst of many disturbances from the people of disobedience, the church came to revival from dying to life during the years from 1993 to 1994. In the following years when I proclaimed the gospel of God at the English Bible Studies at a facility near the University of Alberta, the Lord saved many souls of the nations, including Koreans, Japanese, Chinese, and Germans. We witnessed the phenomena of the Holy Spirit in God's saving many university students and young professionals.

In August 1996, after I fully preached the gospel of God's grace in Edmonton and its environs and facilitated to unite two churches under the care of one pastor, we moved to Vancouver to preach the gospel of Christ to university students.

When I proclaimed the testimony of God's grace in Jesus Christ at the two colleges in Vancouver, several students became believers in the Lord Jesus and experienced eternal life.

Meanwhile, the two churches in Edmonton failed to unite in spirit despite their hard labors for becoming one. Upon hearing that the sheep of my old church were all scattered and were in great distress, I flew to Edmonton to seek and care for the lost in the cold place.

All the flock of my old church greatly rejoiced to see me again. They entreated me to come back as their pastor, but I was not sure it was the will of God. I prayed about it to the Lord all day. A vision appeared to me at night. I beheld the One with the appearance of a man. He was dressed in a brilliant radiance of majestic glory and standing at the door of the hotel room where I was staying. When

I realized that I was standing in the presence of God, I fell down at His feet and worshiped the Lord while fixing my eyes on Him with reverence and fear. Extending a tray with bread on it, the Lord said to me, "Feed the flock." Then the vision went away from me and I woke up. I obeyed the word of the Lord and came back to Edmonton in March 1997.

Not everyone in the community welcomed my second coming to Edmonton. Some took an instant dislike to me and returned evils for my good works for the church of God. To live like the Lord Jesus meant unjust sufferings for me in quietness and trust. While being reviled, I kept entrusting myself to the Lord who judges righteously. My heart was pierced when those who had been drawing near to the Lord through my gospel ministry gave their ears to the evil workers and turned against me. My pain was that I could no longer serve them for their salvation. I endured a great conflict of adversaries and sufferings according to the freedom and power of God.

In the middle of all my persecutions and tribulations during the three years of my second service for my Lord in Edmonton, the Lord accomplished His purpose through my ministry and saved considerable numbers of university students and young professionals by His grace.

In September 1999, a Japanese sister in Christ, who completed her education in Canada and returned to Japan, pleaded me to come to Japan for the gospel. I prayed about the request, but the Lord did not permit it. Instead, the Spirit of the Lord called me to go to a neighboring city, Calgary, Alberta. We obeyed the call of God in October 1999.

On August 3, 2004, after five years of my gospel ministry in Calgary, my wife and I were suddenly guided to see the peoples over the Pacific Ocean during our lunchtime phone conversation about our ministries. We asked, "Where, Lord?" Our instant and simultaneous answer was—Japan.

Reducing all the earthly things of our three-bedroom home to four pieces of luggage to travel to Japan was a formidable task. We sold our house, car, and piano and gave away other things to the needy. When we went to the airport with only two pieces of luggage for each of us, our souls felt a strange, heavenly freedom—the freedom of being released from the burdens of earthly things.

By sight we could not go to Japan. The country occupied Korea by force for thirty-six years. A Japanese Christian asked us with great concerns, "Why Japan among all the countries in the world? Even worse, why Osaka among the many cities in Japan?" He witnessed Japanese discriminating against Koreans residing in Osaka. Japan is also a land with the dangers of earthquakes and *tsunamis* (tidal waves). Besides, we have heard that the missionary works in Japan are very difficult.

By faith we came to Osaka in December 2005 with the mission of evangelizing the people, planting the church of God, and equipping the saints of God for ministries. When we began our ministries, the world stood high and strong against us. One young teacher expressed his displeasure about our missionary works among Japanese by saying, "Why did you come to Japan? You came to the wrong place." He predicted, "You will never make a single Japanese a Christian." In addition, long-time foreign missionaries in Japan warned us that Japan is the graveyard of missionaries. Furthermore, I got sick with food poisoning to the danger of death. We were discouraged by many adversities and burdened by various trials beyond our strength in the early months of 2006.

When we proclaimed the gospel of God to the people in Osaka and the neighboring cities of Kyoto, Kobe, and Wakayama, most of them rejected the offer of salvation from God and said, "I'm a Japanese. (Japanese were proud of being an economically mighty nation next to the United States.) I'm a Buddhist. I don't need the God of Westerners. I'm happy now. And I don't want to change my status quo."

In the midst of all our difficulties and discouragements, the Lord God opened for us a door for His gospel through Kyoko and Tadashi Shinyama. When we boldly testified by the power of the Holy Spirit that Jesus is the Christ, the Son of God, many Japanese came to our ministries. Among them were young men and women who were suffering from depression. At the youthful ages of their twenties and thirties, they were sinking into the deep pit of darkness and despair. Those in their fifties knew the power of money but had no power to forgive others. They were rich in the world but were dying in poverty without the life of God. God brought a total of 104 people to our personal ministries and did His wonders to them during the period from April 2006 to October 2008. We witnessed the blind receive sight, the captives are released to freedom, the weak become strong, the poor become rich, and the perishing are saved to the kingdom of God. We served them for their faith in the risen Christ Jesus and equipped them for good works in our two churches and other churches.

On October 30, 2008, after completing our term of service in Japan, we returned to Canada with joy and thanks. Our hearts are filled with many wonderful memories in Japan. One is that we used to go to the public square of Kyobashi train station on our way home and dance *Awa Odori* of Tokushima, Japan, in the celebration of God's saving a precious Japanese soul. We give thanks to the Lord our God for all the Southern Baptist churches who supported us with finance and prayers.

To Love and Serve Our Neighbors

The Lord our Savior purified our hearts for a sincere love of our neighbors. The love of God from our purified hearts is warm, and we fervently love our neighbors. The abounding grace of God opened the dams of our hearts wide, so that the love of God flows freely to others. It is boundless, limitless, and endless. The flood of love gushes forth from our hearts to our neighbors. We freely unleash our love from our unhindered, wide-open hearts and give of our lives liberally for the good of others.

Though we are free from our neighbors, we use our freedom in the Holy Spirit to serve them through love. Like the Lord Jesus, we freely deny ourselves to serve others. We lay aside our personal freedom, privileges, rights, and interests for those of others.

Christians, who were freed from the laws of the world to the grace of God, can do great things with the power and freedom in the Holy Spirit. We go beyond ourselves to seek the good of our neighbors and exceed all the bounds and limits set by the world. For example, we mow the lawns on our neighbors' properties and remove the snow on the sidewalks in our community. We have the power and freedom to love and serve even our enemies.

The Christian husband with the Holy Spirit has the authority and freedom to love and serve his wife, whereas a man of the flesh is weak and selfish. The husband without the Holy Spirit has no power or freedom to love his wife, as he should. The believing wife with the power of God freely and joyfully obeys and serves her husband, as she does the Lord. A natural wife cannot obey her own husband, as she ought to.

Formerly I was weak through the weakness of the flesh and was under the bondage of selfishness. I desired to be loved and served. Now the Holy Spirit of love and freedom controls me. I live no longer for myself but for my neighbors. I am ready to surrender myself and serve others. And I freely give my life, time, and possessions to meet their needs, and toil for their good.

To Live Godly and Righteously

Christ Jesus set us free to live not for the lusts of man but for the will of God. We are free to order our lives according to the purpose and grace of God in Jesus Christ. We freely present our bodies to God for godliness and righteousness, resulting in sanctification and glorification.

Man's freedom in the world results in sin and death; it is false freedom. It is terrible freedom—freedom to sin, die, and go to hell. The Christian freedom in the Holy Spirit is true freedom; its outcome is sanctification, life, and heaven. We Christians walk by the Holy Spirit, not by the lusts of the flesh. We can do with the power of God the things that our souls please.

Truly, I am free! Formerly I loved my freedom and lived in captivity, but now I obey the Lord my God gladly and find the freedom in the Holy Spirit. My life in the true, glorious freedom results in righteousness and godliness. The Holy Spirit sanctifies me to my Lord, and the glory of God fills my soul. I see the life and glory of God daily.

9. Riches

The Rich Qualities of Eternal Life
 The Love of God
 The Peace of God
 The Joy of God

The Rich Quantities of Eternal Life
 Prosperity
 The Abundance of All Things
 The Good Life

The Lord God blesses His people with the promised life in Christ Jesus. At the era of the Old Testament of the Bible, the God of Israel distinguished the holy nation from all other nations and gave His people the rich, good land of Canaan overflowing with milk and honey for a possession. Now He gives eternal life to the believers in Jesus Christ. We the saints have inherited the riches of God's life and possess everything pertaining to life and godliness. We received the Holy Spirit and have eternal life. The life of God is the rich, good life flowing with the righteousness, love, peace, and joy in the Holy Spirit.

The Rich Qualities of Eternal Life

The Love of God

The object of man's love is what is lovely and lovable. In order to be loved by others, people do their best to look attractive with beautification. On the contrary, the love of God that appeared through the cross of Jesus was for the unlovely and unlovable. We were sinners and were not attractive at all before God, but still He loved us. He is love. His love is so rich that He can love the poor sinners of wretchedness and misery. We were hostile and disobedient as enemies. And also, human love has no power to love those who are different in skin color, culture, social status, and religion. It is difficult for us to love those who hate

136

us. But the Holy Spirit of love gives us the power of God to love the different people. Christians with the Holy Spirit love not because of natural attraction of the beloved but despite of unattractiveness and unworthiness. We do not fall in love but overcome all things with the love and power in the Holy Spirit. We love all people, including orphans, widows, strangers, those who hate us for no reason, and those who mistreat us. The love of God is so rich and powerful that we can love even our enemies.

Whenever I watched the railroads in Japan, I praised the Lord my God for His love for me. During the Second World War, Japanese took my father as a forced laborer from the occupied Korea to Japan. After sixty years, I came to Japan as a missionary of God to deliver Japanese from their slavery to sin and death, and for them to make peace with God. While watching the railroads that carried my father to somewhere in Japan to support the War, I worshiped the Lord my God with my heart full of emotions. I learned to love Japanese from my Lord who loved me and died on the cross for my sin.

The objective of man's love is for self. Many people love others, feed and fatten them to eat their fat. But the love of God is not for the lover but for the good of the beloved. Unselfish love blesses and edifies the beloved. True love is expressed not merely in emotions and words but also in the actions of self-sacrifice. God did not spare His only Son and gave Him up for sinners. The Lord cleansed our sins by His blood for us to be pure. He has sanctified us by His Spirit, so that we might be holy and have the life and glory of God. Christian love labors, costs, and gives. We pour all things on the beloved freely.

We with the Holy Spirit are able to love our neighbors as ourselves. We have purified hearts and have intimate fellowship with the people of God in brotherly love. Christian husbands love their wives, as they do their own bodies, nourishing and cherishing them. Believing husbands and wives submit to each other and give themselves for each other with the love of God. The loving people of God edify one another and sense oneness with God and His people.

The Peace of God

The peace of God is not like the peace that the world gives. The peace of the world can be disturbed by the weather of the world—namely, clouds, winds, rains, snows, and storms. But the peace of God overcomes the weather of the world; it is the power of God. We Christians have many trials and tribulations in the world, but we have peace in our souls since the Lord our God is our peacekeeper. The peace of God guards our hearts with His power from the anxieties and worries of the world. We overcome the tribulations in the world by God's peace. And we enjoy the peace of God in the middle of our trials and tragedies. We live in security from all our enemies within and around us and from the harassment and attacks of Satan and sin. We have no fear of evil, for the Lord is our protector. Indeed, God's peace is the power of God making peace with ourselves, with the world, and with God. The God of peace gives the security of heaven to our souls. We have peace with others and feel a profound sense of rest.

God's peace is much more than the tranquility of graveyards, deep mountains, or sanctuaries built with human hands. It is more than the absence of conflicts. At the times of my ignorance, I thought I had to do nothing to have peace and rest. I slept in late on the weekends and sat in front of TV late in the evening to have rest in inactivity. But I could not refresh or renew myself through the idleness. Rather, I became more tired. My rest without recreation and renewal increased boredom and fatigue to my body and soul. Through my laziness, I entered sloth (negative pressure). Under the depressing burden of inaction, I became depressed. The more I was inactive, the more my soul was falling into despondency. My soul could not find peace and rest in inactivity but rather found restlessness and insecurity like a prisoner condemned to death. The prisoner does nothing in his cell, yet cannot find peace and rest for his soul. Sinners do not know the peace and rest of God.

We enter the peace and rest of heaven when we do the work of believing in the Lord of rest. The believers become refreshed and renewed by doing activities by the Holy Spirit through Jesus Christ. After completing the work of creation, the Lord God rested from

His work with joy and satisfaction. His rest is not retirement from work. Until today, including the Sabbath days, weekends, holidays, and Sundays, He has been doing the work of providence in His grace. Likewise, Christian peace and rest are not inaction or retirement. We find peace and rest for our souls in recreational and providential activities. We enjoy our works for the Lord and others. We ceaselessly perform our services to the glory of God in the Holy Spirit of peace. On Sundays we are busy meeting the needs of others in the grace of God. Through active services for the Lord and others, we enter the peace and rest of heaven from the conflicts and stresses in the world. In the Lord, we enjoy peace and rest for our souls and bodies from all our works in the world.

The Joy of God

The believers in the Lord Jesus have the joy in the Holy Spirit. There is the fullness of joy in the presence of God. The mere thought of Jesus Christ fills my heart with joy; the Lord Jesus is joy. We rejoice in the truth of God. Christian joy is the joy of God's salvation in Christ Jesus. Formerly our lots were death in hell. Now we are raised from perishing to the life of God in holiness and glory.

We the saints of God exult in the hope of God's glory, as a bride rejoices in the hope of presenting herself to her groom in all her glory. We look at the glory that is to be brought to us at the revelation of our Savior Jesus.

Christian joy is the power of God overcoming trials and sufferings. We rejoice with the joy of God when we encounter various trials. Our souls greatly rejoice, even though we have sufferings for the Lord. The joy in the Holy Spirit transcends our present circumstances. The Lord comforts us in our sufferings. Paul, an apostle of Jesus Christ, found this joy in his sufferings for the Lord. He suffered frequent imprisonment, many beatings, stoning, shipwreck, hunger and thirst, sleeplessness, and the dangers of death. Yet he rejoiced with the joy in the Holy Spirit.

The Rich Quantities of Eternal Life

Prosperity

Blessed are we who walk the way of Jesus Christ, because the Lord God prospers our ways to have life in abundance. The life of God is the power of God to prosper. As the Lord of grace multiplies His life in our souls, our heartlands produce the good fruit of the Holy Spirit. We have all things in abundance for life and godliness.

The Abundance of All Things

The saints of God are like fruitful trees at harvest time. We have the rich life overflowing with the love, peace, and joy of God. We enjoy the heavenly standard of living and delight ourselves in the luxurious life. Our yearning for life and prosperity is fulfilled and our lives are meaningful. We sense the usefulness and fulfillment of our lives.

Once we tried to fill the eternal void in our hearts with the things of the world. We ate the produce of earth, but still were hungry for life. We drank strange liquids, smoke, and pleasures, yet we were thirsty for life. We gained the world, but still our lives were empty. In fact, the more we gained the things of the world, the more we became hungry and thirsty. So, we wanted more and more of the world to be satisfied.

Now we have the riches of eternal life in Jesus Christ. He is our satisfaction. Our God has filled the eternity in our hearts with the Holy Spirit of life. The Lord has filled our hungry souls with the good things of the Holy Spirit; He has satisfied our thirsty souls with the living water of heaven. We no longer hunger or thirst, for the Holy Spirit gives us eternal life.

The man of the Bible, Psalm 23 said, "The Lord is my shepherd, I shall not be in want. My cup overflows." He was satisfied not because his circumstances in the world were perfect. He had his enemies chasing after his life; he walked through the valley of the shadow of death. Yet his soul overflowed with the righteousness and peace of God in abundance.

By the grace of God, I became poor in earthly things to make others rich with eternal life. Throughout the years of poverty in the course of my ministry for the Lord, we have always had sufficiency for all the necessities of life—heavenly and earthly things. Our Father in heaven has provided for all our needs (church's and family's) according to His riches. We have not lacked a thing. He has fed us, covered us, and supplied all our necessities. The ancient story of the Lord's providing food and drink for the prophet Elijah through ravens during a drought is our story. The word of the Lord in the Bible, Matthew 6:33 saying, "But seek first his kingdom and his righteousness, and all these things will be given to you as well." is our experience and testimony.

When the Holy Spirit fills me, the other things of the world are unnecessary. My Lord Jesus gives me the new desires and appetites for the things of the Holy Spirit. I eat the food for eternal life day and night, and the life of God fills my soul and my belly. The love, peace, and joy in the Holy Spirit flows out of my soul. I sense the life of God filling my body and taste His peace in my mouth day by day. Oh, the fresh, sweet taste of eternal life! My soul rejoices in the blessed life of God. I sing the joyous songs of praise and thanksgiving to the God of my salvation. My God clothes me with the beautiful robe of His righteousness and covers my nakedness with the glory of His life. And I delight myself in the abundance of heavenly things. Having the riches of God's life, I do not lack for anything in my life.

The Good Life

Experiencing the riches of God's life in Jesus Christ, we rejoice with inexpressible joy by saying, "Life is very good!" The life of God is heavenly. When our souls overflow with eternal life, we are fully satisfied and know that we have the good life. We sense the good will of God for us and bless the Lord our God for the good life that He has given us through His Son Jesus Christ. Thanks be to God for His abounding grace.

The saints of God enter the paradise of God.

10. Paradise

The Presence of God

The Garden of God

The Kingdom of God

In the beginning of the world, the Lord God was with His people in the Garden of Eden. During the age of the Old Testament of the Bible, God dwelled among His people and met with them in the tabernacle and later in the Temple of God in Jerusalem. Now in the age of the new creation in Jesus Christ, God has recreated the wilderness of sin and death into the paradise of God. The saints of God enter the presence of God, possess the garden of God, and see the kingdom of God.

The Presence of God

The Son of God Jesus came down to the world out of heaven from God with His kingdom, power, and glory. The glory of God fills the new world. Behold, the Lord God is in the midst of His people. We the believers are His people. In the presence of His glory, our God dwells among us and meets with us. The saints of God enter the holy place. In the light of God's glory, we are filled with the knowledge of the Lord our God. We know Him just as He is. This world perishes from the presence of God, and there are no longer the things of this world, such as sin, death, darkness, tears, pain, and mourning.

Formerly I was lost in the wilderness of sin and death, far from the Lord God, but now I enter the presence of God, the true sanctuary of heaven. All things are new; I see the new world. I was once perishing in a desert in the wilderness, but now I am standing in the presence of God's glory with great joy.

How glorious is the presence of God! All is His glory. My soul has longed to dwell in the holy place. Now I enter His presence day and night. The presence of God is my dwelling place; I am home with the Lord my God. I will dwell in the sanctuary of God forever.

The holy place of God's presence is the place of worship and service. We the holy priests of God stand before Him and minister to His glory. Our eyes are fixed on the Lord in adoration and our hearts worship Him. We continue to offer up the sacrifices of praise and thanksgiving to our God by the Holy Spirit through Jesus Christ.

The Lord God was among us at the church in Edmonton. He called His people from the nations of the world and made one body. The dividing walls of the barriers separating peoples passed away in the presence of God; we had fellowship with the Lord God and His saints. There were no foreigners or strangers in the family of God. It was beautiful for the brothers and sisters in Christ to dwell together in unity. The light of God's glory illumined us; there was no longer any darkness in our dwelling place. We could see the glory of God in the faces of the saints. Selfish ambition, jealousy, and parties fled away, and there were oneness, sharing, and edifying. As the peace and joy of the Holy Spirit overflowed in our congregation, we rejoiced together.

The presence of God is essential to the life of God's people. In His presence, God sanctifies His people from all other peoples of the world. There He meets us and blesses us. He protects us from our enemies and dangers. On the day of trouble, He is our sanctuary. How blessed are those who dwell in the sanctuary of God! God's presence is the garden of God.

The Garden of God

God gives us the garden of God as an inheritance. We live in the garden of God, our homeland, which supply abundantly to our lives. Here we have the life of God's blessing and bliss. We live in the heavenly wonderland. There is only life, prosperity, and contentment. Death and adversity are the things of the past.

The river of life flows out of the presence of God and waters our heartlands to have life. There is no drought, famine, or emptiness on our heartlands anymore. The living water is our drink. Whatever we do, we prosper. We no longer thirst for life.

There is the tree of life in our heartlands, always yielding the fruit of life abundantly. The living fruit is beautiful to our sight and is good for our food. We eat the fruit of life to the full and are satisfied with the good life of God. There is no longer hunger for life.

The mighty river of the Holy Spirit flows in my heartland, watering and renewing my life. The Lord transformed my heartland from the desert into the garden of God. Now the tree of the Holy Spirit grows there and yields the good fruit of life in abundance. I am old and my hair is grey, yet my life has fruitful seasons. My soul eats the fruit of righteousness, peace, love, and joy, and is satisfied. The Lord has settled me down in His garden to enjoy His blessing. He amply supplies all my needs for life and peace. My desires are fully met; I am not in want.

The garden of God is a life of peace and rest. In the garden of God, we have peace with God, with ourselves, with the world, and with people. The Lord gives us rest from all our enemies, so that we live in peace and security. We cease from our toils and pains and enter the heavenly rest. The garden of God is also a life of healing. Here we live in wholeness and wellness.

In the garden of God, we walk with the Lord, the Shepherd of our souls. He guides our feet to the way of life and peace. There is no longer wandering, stumbling, or perishing; there are good pathways in the garden of God.

How blessed are we who have the perfect life in the garden of God! We are content with the blissful life. Sing praises to the Lord, because His grace is great. The blessed by God enter the kingdom of God.

The Kingdom of God

The Lord our King Jesus came to us in His heavenly kingdom. He has made us to be a holy country of God. The people of God see and enter into the kingdom of God. The Lord reigns over His people with the eternal grace, power, and glory of God.

While serving the Lord in Edmonton in the years from 1993 to 1999, I had to suffer persecutions by the people of the world for the gospel of Jesus Christ. On the dark days when I was in the valley of reproach and shame, I endured forsakenness and aloneness in the world. In those moments of hardships, I looked up to the Lord my Savior in heaven and saw the glory of God. Behold, I was caught up into heaven from the world of sufferings and entered the country of God, full of glory and peace. There I freely flew with no wings but by the Holy Spirit. Some times later, when I saw this world again, I gave thanks to my Lord for giving me the victory in Him. Through my tribulations and sufferings in the world, I entered the kingdom of God. I saw the true, sovereign country of heaven beyond the circumstances of the world.

The King Jesus gave me His authority and power to rule the world with Him. I did good works to those who mistreated me, prayed for those who reviled me, and blessed those who persecuted me. Through all my sufferings, I kept believing in the Lord God of my salvation and endured to finish my course in Edmonton. Sin and death had no power over me; there was no longer defeat and death.

Praise the Lord our King of sovereign dominion over all powers! The rich and powerful in the world are subdued under the judgment of the Lord. He vindicates the poor and afflicted with His justice. He enforces peace over His people according to His power. While I was making a pastoral visitation to a home of a sick person in Edmonton, a man phoned me with angry voice to come urgently to a cafeteria in downtown. When we sat down in the cafeteria, his body shook with fury and his voice was inflamed with the fire of rage. He poured out his allegations about my ministry. But by the authority of God I did not say a word for my explanation and his understanding. Realizing that the opposing force is not the man sitting before me but the ruler of this world, I lifted up my eyes and gazed intently on the Lord my Savior. He was my vision and my hope in the conflict of kingdoms. I prayed for the kingdom of God to come on us. To my surprise, the man suddenly became calm. He was shameful and apologetic when we stood up from the table. He came to me with the flesh and enmity, but I came to him in the name of the Lord and with the Holy Spirit.

The sovereign Lord ruled us with His kingdom and judged us with His righteousness.

Currently the people of God are in the world but are not of the world. We are aliens and pilgrims in the world. And we seek the kingdom of God, which is a heavenly country and a better one than the ones in the world. We look not at the power and glory in this temporal world but at those in the true, eternal world.

While I am in my earthly dwelling in the world, I have not yet fully entered the kingdom of God. But I clearly see the kingdom of God before me and continue on my pilgrimage to heaven. On the way to my eternal home in the holy city of God, sometimes I walk, sometimes I fall, and sometimes I fly.

On the glorious day of the Lord when He makes me stand in His presence eternally, I will end my pilgrimage to heaven through the world. The Lord my God will give me the paradise of God, which is reserved in heaven for His saints.

Summary of Parts Three and Four

The human tragedy of perishing in sin and death is not the end of human story. The death and resurrection of Jesus Christ proves the certainty of a new life after death. We once were perishing into hell, but now we have been raised to eternal life. The destination of man is the life and glory of God. Everyone who believes in the word of God, Jesus Christ has eternal life. We the living with the Holy Spirit enter heaven. The way of God to eternal life and heaven is Jesus Christ. By believing in Jesus Christ, we have eternal life; through Jesus Christ, we enter heaven.

The Lord God does His wonders for the believers. He saves us by delivering from the manifold troubles in the world and then giving His life. We the born of the flesh became the children of God born by the Holy Spirit through Jesus Christ. We are the people of God; the Lord is our God. We love, worship, and serve the Lord our God with all our hearts and lives.

We walk in the way of Jesus Christ by the power of the Holy Spirit. The way of God leads us to the freedom in the Holy Spirit. We the saints of God inherit the riches of eternal life and enter the paradise of God.

Conclusions and Recommendation

This book comes to the following conclusions:

1. Jesus Christ is the way to God, eternal life, and heaven. Through Him we inherit eternal life and enter heaven; therefore, we must come to Him to receive the gift of God.

2. People respond to Jesus Christ with either belief or unbelief. When we repent and turn to the Son of God lifted up on the cross and behold His glory, we believe in Him and have eternal life. But if we disobey the word of God, we will surely perish.

3. There are two ways before us for our pilgrimage to heaven. One is the right way of God in Jesus Christ; the other, the wrong way of man in the world. Man's way in the world appears inviting, since it is broad and easy. Most people journey along the popular way, but it leads to hell. On the other hand, the way of God in Jesus Christ seems narrow and hard, because it is the way of the cross. There are persecutions and sufferings in the way. We must die and rise with Jesus Christ to enter heaven. This is the reason why only a minority enters heaven.

4. The living in the Lord Jesus enter heaven; the dead in sin enter hell.

As I turn and look back over the seventy years of my pilgrimage to heaven through the world, I see the mountains, the valleys, the desert, and the paradise that I have traveled. My journey has been attended with both the peril of perishing and the glory of eternal life. Perishing in the abyss of hell lies behind; the promised life of God in heaven lies ahead. I clearly see the turning point of my pilgrimage to heaven. It is the point where I listened to the message of the cross of Jesus and turned from my sinful and perishing way to behold the Son of God, our Savior. I can testify to you that Jesus Christ is the way to eternal life and heaven.

Consider Jesus Christ. God has been calling you in the name of Jesus. He was lifted up high on the cross, as you yourself know. Turn your eyes to the Lord and Savior Jesus on the cross. This crucified Jesus rose again from the dead and ascended into heaven. Behold the Son of God and see His glory, and you will believe in Him, have eternal life, and enter heaven.

Now, may the grace and truth of God be with you for your safe pilgrimage to heaven. Amen.

CPSIA information can be obtained at www.ICGtesting.com
Printed in the USA
LVOW050135140313

324152LV00003B/5/P